HARDWIRING
NEW LEADERSHIP
HABITS

HARDWIRING
NEW LEADERSHIP
HABITS

DOES DEVELOPMENT DEVELOP?

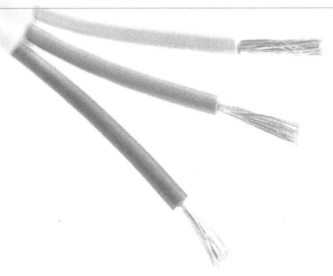

DICK DANIELS

Leadership
Development Group

DEDICATION

Hardwiring New Leadership Habits
is dedicated to the every-day supervisor, manager, or leader
who is committed to developing their character
and competence in order to expand their capacity to lead
at higher levels of organizational complexity.

Leadership development represents an investment in developing supervisors, managers, and leaders at their point of greatest need, and connecting them to the organization's greatest opportunities. These amazing leaders contribute to building a developmental culture that invests in every team member at all levels of the organization. They lead the way in serving each direct report with the resources needed to be successful. They both take the blame and give the credit. They allow for the teachable moments that come from failure. They model the values that define the culture of how every team member works together and how they treat vendors, customers, investors, and competitors. They end each day knowing that they did their best to serve the needs of their organization. They are ready to return tomorrow and lead incrementally better than yesterday. Follow the insights in the fictional story that follows. Perhaps the insights and conclusions have application to your organization and your commitment to develop leaders at every level.

Powerful!

Dr. Daniels' latest book

is engaging, well-researched,

and strikes at the heart of

why so many companies

lack great employee

development efforts.

Hardwiring New Leadership Habits

is the ultimate guide to help

you create the employee

investment your company needs

for long-term success!

—MARSHALL GOLDSMITH

is the *Thinkers50* #1 Executive Coach and
New York Times bestselling author of *The Earned Life*,
Triggers, and *What Got You Here Won't Get You There*.
Founder, The Marshall Goldsmith Group and
the Stakeholder Centered Coaching methodology.

TABLE OF CONTENTS

HARDWIRE CONNECTION #8
AVOID TRIPPING THE TEN CIRCUIT BREAKERS

HARDWIRE CONNECTION #9
A COMPARATIVE CASE STUDY

HARDWIRE CONNECTION #10
DOES DEVELOPMENT DEVELOP?

*Your organization's capacity
for leadership development
determines its capacity to achieve
today's productive potential.*

*Your individual capacity to hardwire
new leadership habits determines
your capacity to lead at higher levels
of organizational complexity.*

INTRODUCTION

FOLLOW THE MONEY

INTRODUCTION—
FOLLOW THE MONEY

OUR FICTIONAL STORY represents the reality within many organizations committed to leadership development. Look for the applicable insights as the story is told through the eyes of one member of the C-Suite team at Global Organization Resources Inc. It all started when Suzanne walked into the conference room, grabbed coffee, and personally greeted each team member before sitting at the head of the board room table. She gathered her C-Suite colleagues, of which I was one, for our annual three-day offsite. It was time to do our collaborative strategic thinking session. These three days were the most critical in prioritizing and aligning the work going forward at Global Organization Resources Inc. (GOR).

The team had done this before. Suzanne was a great CEO. Our homework, in preparation for the offsite, was to analyze the most relevant data from all angles. This included the latest information and metrics about the industry, market, customer, competition, employees, and technology. Our assignment was to look for the story in the numbers.

Our task in this meeting was to come to agreement. What is the main theme? What are the subpoints in the story? What are the side-bars and footnotes? What details are irrelevant? Once it was clear, our work in small groups was to synthesize the information to understand GOR's strengths, weaknesses, opportunities, and threats.

The team's synthesis work included a reality check of our current state with an eye on where we would need to be in "x" months, making it non-negotiable that we would find a way to reach that reality.

Then it happened. It was the awkward moment we all knew was coming. Suzanne posed the five questions. We repeated them in our minds, word for word, while she asked each one. These were the five things that kept us awake at night the entire week before the offsite.

1. The Context Question—**What did we used to do?**
   Those who had been at the company the longest were the best at answering this question.

2. The Reality Question—**What are we doing today?**
   We all had our own piece to the organizational puzzle.

3. The Change Question—**What should we be doing differently?** That's where we learned how to have healthy team conflict.

4. The Priority Question—**What should we be doing next?**
   We never lacked for ideas. The challenge was prioritizing the longer list to our top ten and then to our top three.

5. The Letting Go Question—**What should we stop doing?**
   We all had our "sacred cows," the things we would not want to let go. Sunsetting past initiatives was, perhaps, the most difficult of all our discussions and decisions.

Hopefully those questions will help you understand the dynamics, the dilemmas, and the difficult decisions we faced during the next seventy-two hours. Shawna was our appointed icebreaker. She got us started with a lightning round of crazy questions. What's your favorite color? Why? With whom is your most troubled family relationship? Yes, we needed the courage to be vulnerable, but that is how well we trusted and knew each other. What is one of the funniest moments of your life? What experience continues to influence the person you are today?

Well, this year, Shawna's icebreaker started with five pictures of different people in different situations with different emotional expressions. Her question: Which picture is most representative of you at this point in your life? She clarified with a distinction among the situation, the person, or the perceived emotion. Any of the three were fair game in answering.

Needless to say, we got deep really quickly. In my opinion, this was always the highlight of each annual offsite. It pulled us together. It forced us to be honest and open in the spirit of confidentiality. Whatever was said at the offsite, stayed at the offsite. We all agreed.

Day one was a review of what we saw in our individual analysis of the data. Imagine a room decorated on all three walls with flip chart pages and sticky notes. The "Fourth Wall" was our dedicated summary wall. Nothing could be added to that wall that did not pass the standard of consensus. Our first day ended with an early dinner followed by some physical activity we would do to compensate for the hours we sat around the board room table. It wasn't long, but it was intentional.

This particular year, we had a yoga instructor take us though sixty minutes of stretching exercises. The second night, we had three teams of three competing in a series of activities. Everyone had two attempts to putt a golf ball into a small circle, two attempts to make a basket with a basketball at the free throw line, one random draw of five cards from a deck to see who got the best hand, a roll of the dice for the highest combined number, a game of checkers for each one against one of the other teams, and a hopscotch marked on the sidewalk with chalk. We were all timed for our ability to stay within the boxes as we hopped through!

It sounds silly, but the laughter always created one of the most memorable moments for the team. No cameras allowed as the rest of the company already wonders about our shenanigans! In our offsite icebreakers, the winning team was awarded a night of fine dining together along with our significant other. The prize provided enough incentive even for the non-competitive types to get competitive. Unfortunately, my team did not get the most points on evening two this particular year. We decided we all need golf instructions...at least more putting practice!

Day two was what we called our Synthesis Day. The goal was to connect the dots that might clarify what was needed to close the gap between our current state and the future desired state. The identified future goal was elevated on day one as our primary goal and included on the Fourth Wall. That's why we invest this time each year. It's what leads me to the reason for the subtitle for this larger hardwire connection: *Does Development Develop?* It's a question that must be asked!

We have prided ourselves in being known as a company with a developmental culture. We believe in and are committed to developing the people who work here. It has been an amazing retention strategy, but it also became an attraction strategy. It's one of the reasons I've stayed here in spite of other attractive offers throughout the years.

This is the point when the CFO, usually the quiet one in the corner who's looking over his spreadsheets, made a cameo appearance in our discussion. Wilson was new three years prior. He came from a credentialed background which included an Ivy League MBA and twelve years as a Comptroller with a global competitor. He checked every box in the hiring priorities...until now.

It was mid-morning on the second day of the offsite. Wilson was providing an executive summary of our financial statements including the balance sheet, the income statement, and the cash flow statement.

Then he asked the question that muted the entire room. Actually, it wasn't a question. It was a statement. He said, "When I look at the way we are spending our money to do our business, I think we have some internal expenses that are essential and nonnegotiable. Alongside those costs to do business is the money we spend on developing people. It's the warm, fuzzy expenditures that make us feel better, but they represent a larger percentage of our budget than is typical in our industry. It's three times more than our two largest competitors spend annually." He continued, "I think those funds can be better spent on our new social media strategy to target our new market segments. I believe we can beat our #2 competitor if we play our cards right. I'd like to suggest that this idea get added to the Fourth Wall summary of our conclusions and action steps."

We were totally silent as Wilson doubled down on his sentiment, "I'm not sure development really develops anyone anyway. I'm a numbers person. How can you document that changes actually occur...let alone that they stick?"

I was shocked. We were shocked. Say what? Suzanne, realizing this would involve a dramatic organizational shift, reminded Wilson that nothing gets to the Fourth Wall until we discuss all top ten ideas and then vote on the top three.

Here's the short story of what happened. Wilson's idea made it to the top ten because no one had time to respond with reasonable ideas that contradicted his assumptions. Suzanne stood up before our first round of voting. She knew that this particular idea would be divisive at all levels of employment. She was called to lead, and she stepped up to do so.

"We have been committed to an organizational identity that believes in developing our workforce. It is what distinguishes us from our competition. Wilson has explained a rationale of how our development budget could be used to leverage and maximize our marketing strategy to meet sales goals during the next thirty-six months. The rest of you have pulled me aside or sent texts or emails in opposition to his recommendation. What I would like to suggest is that we pull this idea off the top ten list...for now. In forty-five days, we are going to meet and review all the information on both sides of this decision. In the meantime, Wilson already has his suggestion well thought out."

Suzanne continued, "The framework of his ideas made me realize that we have never articulated the "who, what, when, where, why, and how" in our commitment to developing our workforce. His question stopped me dead in my tracks as I consider how we best invest in our business. Does development develop? And does change last? What happens to those new habits each of us are developing once we get a year or so down the road?"

Suzanne finished with a homework assignment: "So, I want the eight of you to meet and make the case for what we have been doing. Maybe we will find that there isn't a case for development when we sort it all out. If there is, then we will have an understanding of why we are committed to development. Then come back and tell me your story. I want to know the main theme, the subthemes, the sidebars, and the footnotes. You know how I think, so help me see how we know that development develops...if it actually does."

We scheduled a two-hour meeting the following week just to get organized. Suzanne wanted to speak the first five minutes to set the stage before we started. During that meeting, she made two points.

First, "I want to clarify the difference between Return on Investment (ROI) and sustainability. One leads to the other. ROI is the big umbrella topic. Sustainability of change contributes to the Return On Investment of our development efforts with each employee. If we help supervisors, managers, and leaders develop new ways of leading that enhance their effectiveness and efficiency, then it will impact the organizational ROI."

Second, "The task I want you to focus on is sustainability. If you can document how hardwiring happens, then we will let our number's people calculate the data and connect the dots to the ROI before the executive team meets in forty-five days. The calculation is not your skill set or your assignment. We all know it's easier to start the development journey in all of our program initiatives, than it is for each individual to apply their learning in a way that sustains their changes. So, if you can bring greater clarity to how we anchor change and development, then it validates our investment in each employee at every level of our company. We want to know if development really does develop!"

Fast forward to our two hours in planning. We identified our model for analysis to develop the C-Suite proposal called "Hardwiring New Leadership Habits." There was one idea for each of us to research. We worked in two teams with four in each team for review, discussion, and revision of our individual assignments. What follows is the detail of our progress. As the reader, we'd like to invite you to participate in the analysis of our work. What have we missed? What have we overstated? What bias is evident in our group-think tendency? Yes, we looked for the hardwire connections in the most relevant data. We hoped the synthesis would lead us to some key hardwired connections that we could add to the Fourth Wall when we met with the entire team, including Wilson, our skeptical CFO. One guiding thought before you formulate your critique of our collective work: There is more to the story than just following the money. Here is a list of our individual assignments:

HARDWIRE CONNECTION #1:
Pathways to Development: How does development begin?

HARDWIRE CONNECTION #2:
Organizational Enablers: What is needed to support development?

HARDWIRE CONNECTION #3:
The Who's Who Matrix: Who are we focused on?

HARDWIRE CONNECTION #4:

It All Happens on Three Levels: Is there an
organizational structure that fosters development?

HARDWIRE CONNECTION #5:

When Learning is Applied: How does an individual
translate learning into new leadership habits?

HARDWIRE CONNECTION #6:

Connecting Three Wires: What is needed to
strengthen the hardwiring of new leadership
habits?

HARDWIRE CONNECTION #7:

Perfection or Progress: Are the development
expectations realistic?

HARDWIRE CONNECTION #8:

Avoid Tripping the Ten Circuit Breakers: Are there
connection problems that disrupt development?

HARDWIRE CONNECTION #9:

A Comparative Case Study: Can Leaders Move from
Operations to Strategy?

HARDWIRE CONNECTION #10:

Does Development Develop? Are new habits
sustainable?

Developmental organizations
make developmental teams possible.
Developmental teams make
developing individuals possible.

When all three intersect and
work together toward the same
mission, vision, and values, then
the probability of hardwiring new
leadership habits increases.

The organization is critical.
The team is essential.
The individual is non-negotiable.

HARDWIRE CONNECTION #1

HARDWIRE CONNECTION #1— PATHWAYS TO DEVELOPMENT

HOW DOES DEVELOPMENT BEGIN?

IT'S NOT SURPRISING that billions of dollars are being spent annually on leadership development. The actual numbers vary depending on the estimating organization. The significance is staggering. No matter how you look at it, it's a lot of money. No wonder Wilson was questioning the money we were spending on developing our team. Our challenge was understanding and explaining our budgetary line item.

The motivation in developing team members is either proactive or reactive. Companies spend money proactively to move the needle from good to great in specific aspects of one's leadership. There will be areas of leading where individuals are good, but the competency or behavior is so critical to their success that it needs further development.

The other approach is a reactive investment to address problem areas or deficiencies in one's leadership approach. Our assumption is that leadership represents learned competencies. Great leaders never stop growing, so they never stop learning and applying what they learn. Sometimes the reactive initiative is a last attempt to help a team member before deciding whether to retrain, reassign, or release and replace them.

In both cases, reactive or proactive, the motivation represents an investment in developing people at their point of greatest need connected to the organization's greatest opportunities. In our research for Hardwire Connection #1, we identified three pathways explaining why money is spent, how money is spent, and how leaders find ways to grow in specific behaviors or leadership competency areas. It is learning that launches one's development journey.

Lifelong Learners

Type A leaders are driven by a commitment to lifelong learning, often at their own initiative, time, and even expense. They are motivated to improve their leadership skills by their personal reading, time invested in online learning, and/or through in-person leadership training events. Such learning can be customized to meet the specific needs or interests of the individual. In this virtual world, learning opportunities are accessible on a daily basis for those ready to upskill their competencies. The goal is two-fold:

> First, to continue increasing one's effectiveness and efficiency in the work they are currently doing. Second, to add the skills needed for readiness to pursue or to consider a role at a higher level of organizational complexity.

Self-driven learning is of value when it connects work-related developmental needs to learning styles that move the individual incrementally forward. This leads to new habits, the application of those new habits, and the stretching required to lead differently for the long haul. Lisa Lang, Head of People Enablement and Growth for the Americas at Siemens USA said in an article published by the Association of Talent Development, "What individuals learn in school is no longer enough to sustain a career. Learning must be embedded into employee's daily lives at work to facilitate lifelong learning."[1]

Leadership Institutes

Larger organizations are leading the way in creating their own internal leadership institute, academy, or department, generally under the auspices of the human resources department. Part of what they offer includes introductory leadership sessions open to anyone as a way to empower any team member to begin the intentional journey of strengthening their skills. More specifically, they offer some form of a year-long cohort model available by invitation only. In some cases, individuals can apply to be accepted into a new cohort, or in other companies, people must be recommended or sponsored by a more senior leader within the organization.

The curriculum choice is often a mix of buying resources externally and building resources internally. The leader-as-teacher model equips select senior leaders to teach training events within the institute. Not only is this more cost effective, but it also stretches the teaching leader in new ways and hopefully strengthens their credibility in light of their own leadership reputation. These company-based learning and growth opportunities enable the organization to tailor curriculum and learning styles needed to address their internal competency model and to meet the strategic outcomes of the company.

Competency models at each level of leadership help narrow the topical selection of what offerings have relevance and immediate application for supervisors, managers, and leaders. The internal structure and availability of a leadership development process offer the invitation and convenience to any employee to take personal responsibility and initiative to shape their career goals and define a pathway to get there.

Leadership Coaching

The third pathway is coaching. The leader-as-coach model is an approach using internal supervisors, managers, and leaders as coaches for each of their direct reports. It's a way of letting development trickle down throughout the entire organization at all levels of employment. Training of coaching basics is essential to this pathway.

At a more formal coaching level, certified internal coaches are used for mid-level positions, and certified external coaches are used for more senior positions in six- to twelve-month coaching engagements. Coaching is not to be confused with counseling or mentoring because each represents a different nuance of offering helpful insights and support to others. Let's define each one:

> **Coaching** — The International Coaching Federation (ICF) defines coaching as "partnering with clients in a thought-provoking and creative process that inspires them to maximize their personal and professional potential."[2] Coaching is for a specified period of time, generally six to twelve months. It is structured around a few focus areas that address behaviors and competencies. It is measurable in outcomes, and it is addressing the potential for one's future performance and productive potential. Certification is becoming more of an expected standard in the area of coaching. Training in coaching ethics along with supervision by master coaches are part of the ongoing education to enhance the credentials and quality of coaches and the consistency of their methodology in the marketplace.

Mentoring — It takes place when someone with greater life experience, work knowledge, or connections gives advice to someone with less life experience, work knowledge, or connections. It is more informal and can last for a longer duration of time than coaching. Mentors give their personal advice based on their experience. Mentoring is less structured. Certification or licensing are not always required for mentors.

Counseling — It is often retrospective, looking to understand the influence of the past and why it is impacting one's current reality. Counseling is typically a longer duration than coaching or mentoring. The counselor is seen as an authority addressing the client's challenges with professionalism and confidentiality. According to the American Psychological Association, "Counseling psychology is a generalist health service (HPS) specialty in professional psychology that uses a broad range of culturally-informed and culturally-sensitive practices to help people improve their well-being, prevent and alleviate distress and maladjustment, resolve crises, and increase their ability to function better in their lives."[3] Licensing for counselors is required by law.

Final Thoughts

The primary idea in Hardwire Connection #1 regarding leadership development delivery options is this: Learning launches the developmental journey. Assessment and feedback can help focus one's learning more specifically. Wherever new leadership habits are formed, the challenge is one of sustainability. How do we hardwire new leadership habits in order to lead more effectively and efficiently for the long haul? Sustainability in applying what is learned is strengthened when the organization not only values but invests in developing its leaders.

Connections between these two organizational factors will result in one of four possible outcomes.

The invitation for organizations committed to growing leaders is to combine their value of development with their investment in that development. In other words, we need to put our money where our mouth is!

FOURTH WALL CONCLUSION

The analysis in Hardwire Connection #1 brings us closer to understanding how the development journey begins. When a leader has clarity on specific leadership behaviors or competencies that need attention, then the development journey begins through structured learning translated into new habits in how one leads. Learning is where hardwiring begins but learning without application is merely an academic exercise with no meaningful return on investment for the business at large. We are aware that there will always be team members who take advantage of learning opportunities but may never translate that learning into new ways of supervising, managing, and leading. That is one of our challenges going forward. The purpose of learning in our thinking is to continue one's development in order to provide more effective leadership with maximum impact and efficiency. That initial idea in our analysis begins to shape our Fourth Wall Conclusion.

Leadership development

represents an investment

in developing supervisors,

managers, and leaders

at their point of greatest need

connected to the organization's

greatest opportunities.

HARDWIRE CONNECTION #2

ORGANIZATIONAL ENABLERS

What is needed to support development?

» The Leadership Development Mission

» The Leadership Development Vision

» The Leadership Development Values

» Connecting the Dots: Mission, Vision, and Values

» The Rest of the Organizational Enabler Story

» Final Thoughts

» Fourth Wall Conclusion

HARDWIRE CONNECTION #2—
ORGANIZATIONAL ENABLERS

MISSION, VISION, AND VALUES are foundational in any organization. These three enablers shape the context of our shared work. They provide boundaries within which we can create a development culture and then wrestle with the question of sustainability in hardwiring new leadership habits. They provide a collective picture of "us" at our best, and they tell the story of our productive potential if we worked in near-perfect performance with continuous mutual alignment.

It was helpful for our C-Suite team at Global Organization Resources Inc. to go back to these basics and review our organizational declarations of:

» What we do (Mission)
» What it's leading to (Vision)
» How we do it (Values)

It was a reality check when our team did an honest assessment and admitted the gap between the ideal pictured in the mission, vision, and value statements compared to the reality of our daily work life. The organizational challenge is finding continual ways to shorten the distance between the defined ideal and the reality of our imperfections.

Every day we walk past the plaque on the lobby wall that reminds us of who we are and who we are becoming. It's on the home page of our website when we log in to work. We are better at seeing the growth opportunities needed in others before we see what needs growth and development in ourselves! We all work with some form of baggage that comes out of our past or present experiences, failures, life stressors, or the random bad days that come with disagreements at home, not feeling well, gnarly traffic, too many meetings, a toxic co-worker, and more!

Our shared imperfections keep us from living out the ideal culture described in Hardwire Connection #1. It's no wonder we need to focus on the development of leadership behaviors and competencies. Even though we all may be good at what we do, there is opportunity and a need for us to get better individually and collectively in order to accomplish the daily mission, live out our values, and achieve our ultimate vision.

It was decided to start with a review of what mission, vision, and values represent at the organizational level and then apply these terms specifically to our discussion of leadership development and, finally, to consider how it influences the sustainability of new habits. Let's consider both sides of this topic: The organization and then leadership development within the organization.

» The Macro Perspective. The more intentional we are in closing the organizational gap between culture (ideal) and climate (reality), the more we are apt to achieve the productive potential of the company on the way to reaching the preferred future about which we cast a vision.

» The Micro Perspective. The more intentional we are in closing the leadership development gap between value and investment, the more we will develop leaders at every level and establish a pipeline with bench strength for succession planning in each critical role within the organization.

The Organizational *Mission.* It offers clarity on why GOR Inc. exists. It defines our company's business, its objectives, and its approach to achieving those objectives. Mission is our reason for being. It describes what we do day in and day out when every team member lives out their full potential and capacity in each role assignment.

The Organizational *Vision.* It is our inspired statement that continually re-casts a shared picture of what our organization is becoming. Vision stretches the organization's capacity and its self-image, giving shape and direction to its future. Vision is a motivational forecast of what the company is headed toward as it lives out the daily mission.

The Organizational *Values.* These are the guiding beliefs that influence how every team member thinks, talks, and behaves while living out the mission on the way to achieving the vision. Values translate into service standards. When you "behavioralize" your values, you provide a word picture of what each idea looks like in daily work life. Values provide common language of how we agree to work together with other employees, vendors, customers, and investors.

Connecting the Dots. Our mission, vision, and values clarify the context which ultimately raises the question of how we hardwire new leadership habits along the way. Our C-Suite's proposal was an alternative understanding to the challenge from our CFO, Wilson. His assumption is that the bottom line is our only budgetary metric when considering how we spend money in the development of supervisors, managers, and leaders at every level in the organization.

As CFO, Wilson meant well, but we felt he was biased in his tendency to just follow the money. In Hardwire Connection #2, we were working to apply the organizational mission, vision, values model specifically to our work of leadership development. We were driven by our commitment to incremental change in developing new leadership habits in our supervisors, managers, and leaders. Our company's mission, vision, and value statements are listed below. We believe that these ideas help address our Fourth Wall answers to the question: Does development develop?

The Leadership Development *Mission*

To develop leaders at every level in the entire organization.

> » *Supervisors* who provide lower-level oversight
> of teams of people.

> » *Managers* who provide mid-level oversight
> of teams of people.

> » *Leaders* who provide top-level oversight
> of managers and other leaders.

The roles, competencies, and behaviors can vary among these three levels, but each category needs development opportunities to address specific tasks and competencies that strengthen the oversight role.

People often get promoted because they are tactical and operational, subject-matter experts, but they have never been equipped to supervise, manage, or lead a team. The key phrase in our mission statement is "every level." If you want to hardwire new leadership habits, then do it for all three levels. Only then do you truly have a developmental culture in your company.

Leadership Development *Vision*

To establish a succession planning leadership pipeline from the company's talent pool.

> » If mission is what we do day in and day out, then vision describes what that daily activity is leading to long term.

> » Vision answers the question of what it is we are ultimately trying to accomplish by developing leaders at every level in our organization?

Succession planning usually maps out potential retirement sequences for various key supervisors, managers, and leaders in order to avoid last-minute scrambling and hasty decisions. Succession strategy can also identify plans if a key team member leaves for a new job. As we all know, any extended vacancy in these roles puts the company at risk. Without a cultural value of developing leaders at all organizational levels, it is a challenge to replace key leaders in a timely way with someone who has the skills and readiness to step into that role when the organization needs that role filled.

Companies are investing in developing new leadership habits, not only so people are more effective in their current role, but also to prepare people to move to a higher level of organizational responsibility. This investment contributes to the retention of your best talent.

Leadership Development *Values*

The values in hardwiring new leadership habits include the following:

Character: It is the consistency of who we are when everyone is looking and when no one is looking. The ancient Greek plays helped define the word hypocrite as the actor who is one person on stage but a different person off stage. People of character consistently demonstrate qualities of positive character. Think of the words you would use to describe your ideal neighbor, colleague, or spouse. Your words most likely represent the qualities of positive character. In the workplace, character brings forward the values that define the culture.

Character is summarized in two critical ideas:

1. Integrity is the personal side of character. It's how other people see you in terms of the consistency of who you are publicly and privately.

2. Respect is the interpersonal side of character. It's how you see other people in terms of emotional and social intelligence.

Integrity and respect are the tandem ingredients that result in one's leadership influence in all relationships, internally and externally. Without integrity and respect as your leadership foundation, hardwiring other new leadership habits will be irrelevant.

Competence: Character is about influence, while competence is about effective action. Rather than demonstrating who you are, competence shows what you do and how well you do it. Can you do the job? It is all about the effectiveness and efficiency in regularly doing one's job well. Competence supports the business strategy and results.

One of the toughest leadership transitions is the move from operational leader to strategic leader. Operational experts have a competency mix unique to that role. They are strategic enough, but most of their time is focused on tactical operations. For example, they might spend 20 percent of their time on strategy and 80 percent of their time on operational leadership. When promoted, especially at the SVP, EVP, or C-Suite level, the mix may be closer to 80 percent strategy and 20 percent operational.

The temptation of the former operational leader and now strategic leader is to default to their operational expertise when under stress or pressure. It will happen at times, but if it is the general default pattern, then it becomes a potential career derailer. If the strategic leader can't let go of their past expertise in operations, then it overtakes any skills they have developed in their new strategy role.

Capacity: Capacity has to do with the ability to lead effectively and efficiently, while also showing potential to lead at higher levels of organizational complexity and responsibility. In certain seasons of life, we may have the ability but not the readiness to take on more. Capacity is the preparedness for an opportunity. Readiness is having the bandwidth in one's life to take advantage of that opportunity. Both are necessary!

Careers are all about seasons, and each season in our life has transitions that demand different things of us. All seasons are not equal, and each season may not be the time to take on greater responsibility or a steep learning curve. These seasons could include young children, aging parents, chronic illness in the family, financial stressors, and relationship dysfunctions. We should always seek to hardwire new habits in order to increase our leadership capacity for greater efficiency in current roles or for readiness when the season is right for promotion or an entirely new position.

Cultural Fit: Fit within a team or organization is influenced by one's attitudes, motives, values, preferences, background, experience, education and how closely those align with their organization. Character and competence are foundational to one's fit. We like the person with character but if they lack competence, we don't respect them. We respect the person who is competent, but if they lack qualities of positive character, we don't like them. Consider the four outcomes in connecting character and competence:

From a different perspective, fit is also affected by one's personality and work styles. For example, the toxic team member, the arrogant know-it-all, the constant critic, the performance minimalist, and the individual who brings the worst of personal baggage into the workplace are all examples of people who will not fit any healthy corporate culture. If an individual is not a cultural fit, and we end up not liking or respecting them while they do their job, then new leadership habits will likely not be enough to close the "fit gap."

Connecting the Dots: Mission, Vision, and Values

Mission, vision, and values are interrelated. Collectively, they are "organization enablers." Within each statement, there is intentionality and direction in what we offer to every employee. This can influence our attraction and retention efforts. When each of these enablers dynamically interacts with the other two, it provides an undisputable foundation to our core directional identity. We are committed to practice the development of employees at all levels of the company. Among other advantages, development moves us further and faster to achieve our mission, vision, and values. Some cautions are noteworthy to clarify and distinguish the connection among these organizational enablers.

...**Vision.** Never consider organizational vision without reflecting on organizational mission. Always ask: "What is the mission of our daily activity that leads to accomplish the vision?"

...**Mission.** Never consider organizational mission without reflecting on organizational vision. In light of your preferred future state. Always ask: "What do we need to be doing day in and day out to achieve that inspirational goal of a new tomorrow?"

...**Values.** Never consider values until you can clearly and compellingly cast vision of what your company is becoming while living out the mission.

...**Mission, Vision, and Values.** Never move forward with your mission and vision without reflecting on the values that shape the organizational culture and define the context in which doing the daily mission will achieve the future vision.

...**Fit.** Never consider a key hire without reflecting on "fit." Does this candidate fit the values of the shared organizational culture, indicating how every team member will work with other team members, vendors, customers, and investors? Can this candidate do the job competently? Do they have the personal drive to do it well? Will we like and respect them while they do the job? When fit is missing, development doesn't develop. In other words, development can't repair the gap that exists between your candidate and the organizational culture. It is often said, "Hire hard. Manage easy!"

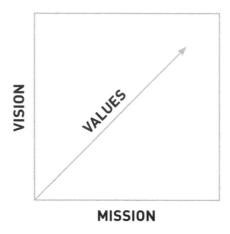

The Rest of the Organizational Enabler Story

Mission, vision, and values rarely, if ever, will change. What continues to change is the strategy, structure, staffing, and systems that provide the organizational capability to live out the mission and values on the way to achieving the vision.

> » Strategy indicates the steps that will get the organization from where it is today to the next benchmark needed to reach the organizational vision.

> » Structure provides the best way to organize the resources of the organization to maximize its productive potential. It's worth noting that structure is a reflection of the strategy. Always ask what structure is needed to accomplish the strategy.

» Staffing models adapt to the structure that is required for the strategy to be successful.

» Systems streamline the organizational approach in optimizing the performance of every team member. Systems align individuals and teams around shared goals and facilitate collaboration across typical functional boundaries.

When the strategy changes to more effectively fulfill the mission and vision, then structure also needs to be reviewed and adjusted to reflect the updated strategy. When structure changes, then staffing should be reviewed and adjusted to reflect the updated structure. When staffing changes, then systems should be reviewed and adjusted to reflect the updated staffing.

All these building blocks of healthy organizational frameworks are dynamic and interrelated. Mission, vision, values, strategy, structure, staffing, and systems are the keys to organizational strength and health. If there is a weak link in any part of that sequence, then it takes time, attention, energy, and resources away from developing employees at any level throughout the entire organization. Or, think of it this way, it takes time, attention, energy, and resources away from achieving the productive potential of the entire organization! Development and productive potential are intricately tied together. One is dependent on the other.

Final Thoughts

When aligned, the mission, vision, and values establish "True North" for every team leader. It enables each supervisor, manager, and leader to be more intentional in what it will take to achieve the strategic outcomes of the organization enhanced by their own continuing development and the development of each direct report. The agenda will vary for each person, but the contribution to each person's continual improvement is the result of a process that identifies specific leadership habits that need their ownership and attention.

The measurement of sustainability in hardwiring new leadership habits includes but is not limited to: 1. Achieving the metrics represented in the daily mission, 2. Making measured progress toward benchmarks needed to reach the vision, and 3. Living out the values with intentionality and accountability in all internal and external work relationships.

» When those results are consistently being demonstrated, then we are closing the *organizational gap* between the culture (our ideal) and the climate (our reality).

» This also provides evidence that we are closing the *leadership development gap* in our value of a developmental culture and our investment in making that value a reality for every employee.

» We will seek to show measured improvement in our achievement of the productive potential of each team member, each team, and the entire organization.

» We will contribute to what is needed to maximize the strategic growth of the company on its way to achieving the vision. That is only possible if we protect the company's potential with a continual pipeline of supervisors, managers, and leaders whose incremental development is equipping them with the ability and readiness to step into new roles at higher levels of organizational complexity and responsibility.

FOURTH WALL CONCLUSION

Hardwire Connection #2 continues our C-Suite team's research and analysis of what is needed to clarify the context of leadership development at Global Organization Resources Inc. We are applying the ideas of mission, vision, and values from an organizational level specifically to our company's work in developing every supervisor, manager, and leader.

The three organizational enablers—mission...vision...values— bring clarity to the work of leadership development. They apply to leaders at every level of the organization. They contribute to an internal pipeline of developing supervisors, managers, and leaders who continue to invest in the strengthening of their competence in order to enhance their own leadership capacity. As leaders model professional growth, they are also investing in the development of each of their direct reports.

Cultural fit is the question to ask long before asking the development question. It is an essential filter to use in the hiring process. It's not just about performance, potential, and personal drive. Hiring also considers one's fit within the culture of how we work together with other employees, vendors, customers, investors, and even competitors. "If we hire you, will we like you (character) and will we also respect you (competence)?" Development never fixes fit. If you don't fit, then hardwiring new leadership habits is a waste of time.

The return on investment from clarifying the mission, vision, and values in leadership development is the long-term protection of the organization's viability in seasons of employee retirement or workforce turnover.

» Mission—We are committed to develop leaders at every level of the company.

» Vision—We have a succession planning pipeline from the company's talent pool.

» Values—We pay attention to character, competence, capacity, and the cultural fit of every team member.

When outstanding values

reinforce a challenging mission

and an inspiring vision,

then you're already far down

the road in achieving

the productive potential

of every team member and

ultimately, the productive potential

of the entire organization.

HARDWIRE CONNECTION #3

THE WHO'S WHO MATRIX

Who are we focused on?

» The New Nine Box Grid

» It's All About Personal Drive

» The Upper Right and the Lower Left

» Final Thoughts

» Fourth Wall Conclusion

HARDWIRE CONNECTION #3— THE WHO'S WHO MATRIX

WHO ARE WE FOCUSED ON?

THE NINE BOX GRID has always been a helpful leadership tool in understanding how to appropriately develop each of our direct reports. On an annual basis, every supervisor, manager, and leader at GOR Inc. charts where they think each of their direct reports are among the nine boxes on the grid. Yes, we are suggesting that you put each of your direct reports in a "box"! The box they end up in determines the agenda for their professional development. This isn't to share with them, but rather for you to be sure you have an accurate picture of where they are at and where they are headed. The new Nine Box Grid helped us think through Hardwire Connection #3 in order to answer the question of who we are focused on in development initiatives.

The New Nine Box Grid

Two of our bigger challenges are how to respond to those in the lower left (low performance and low potential) and how to retain those in the upper right (high performance and high potential). How long do you let team members stay in the lower left, and what do you do to provide opportunities to stretch and grow your high potentials in the upper right?

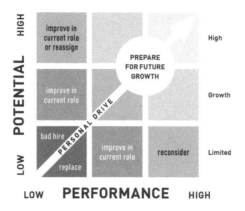

Your message will vary depending on which box each direct report is in. It's the ongoing challenge of leadership. You can't lead each direct report in the same way. Everyone falls into one of three groups: 1. Expectation Exceeders, 2. Expectation Meeters, and 3. Expectation Missers. Development agendas should be focused on what is required to move each group toward the upper right area of the grid. The unanswered question is the degree to which they will engage with your developmental expectation. Performance should have clear metrics to document achievement. Potential is an estimation at best. Are performance and potential enough to determine where development dollars are invested?

It's All About Personal Drive

Traditionally in the HR world, we only think of two Nine Box Grid dimensions needed for organizational investment in leadership development: Performance and Potential. Promotion is often based on meeting expectations in one's current role. That's performance-based career development. Potential always has an eye on a future role asking the question: "How high can you lead?" In a new version of the Nine Box Grid, the Leadership Development Group has added a third dimension: Personal Drive. It is what distinguishes those who merely settle from those who truly excel in their work. Those with high personal drive can become your high potentials and maybe your high performers who consistently exceed expectations.

> » Performance is the degree to which direct reports meet expectations.

> » Potential is the possibility of direct reports exceeding expectations.

> » Personal Drive is one's intensity and intentionality in closing the gap between performance and potential.

The Nine Box Grid is foundational to our developmental culture at GOR Inc. to answer the question: Who is the ideal target for the development and hardwiring of new leadership habits? It's those in the upper right area of the grid! It doesn't ignore the others but simply prioritizes our A, B, and C players. The A players are those with exceptional performance and anticipated potential who have the drive to achieve high levels of organizational responsibility as supervisors, managers, or leaders. Hardwiring their new leadership habits may be easier than those in the upper left or lower right.

The Upper Right and Lower Left

Hardwire Connection #3 raises the questions of intentionality and focus on development. Direct reports are all in various places on the Nine Box Grid, which implies that each one has a different development agenda. The following four messages provide a plan for leaders to develop direct reports in each corner of the Nine Box Grid.

1. Low Performers/Low Potential. Team members in the lower left need a message of direction to alert them to unacceptable performance.

2. High Performers/Low Potential. Team members in the lower right need a message of affirmation to challenge them to continue to perform beyond expectations.

3. Low Performers/High Potential. Team members in the upper left need a message of correction to determine if they can and will improve performance.

4. High Performers/High Potential. Team members in the upper right need a message of expectation to challenge and reward their capacity in setting a new standard for best practice performance.

Final Thoughts

The investment in each of the four combinations above will invite every team member to continue their professional development toward greater productivity, engagement, satisfaction, and retention. It also provides an appropriate way to identify and then address those in the lower left who consistently are content to underperform and may need to be released and replaced. When they are allowed to underperform, it negatively impacts everyone else and decreases the productive potential of the team. Leveling the playing field always takes the team average down and never up.

FOURTH WALL CONCLUSION

As we considered performance, potential, and personal drive related to one's developmental potential in Hardwire Connection #3, our team came to the following insights and conclusions:

» For those in the lower left of the New Nine Box Grid, development may not develop them. If it doesn't, then the difficult question of whether to release and replace them confronts the leader for the sake of the rest of the team. Not dealing with the lower left has a negative impact on the development of every other team member.

» For those in the middle of the grid or in the upper right, the potential for development leading to higher levels of responsibility is measured by the combination of past performance, perceived future potential, and especially personal drive.

» Performance that exceeds expectations and potential that allows one to stand out is based, in part, on the perceptions of others. The validity of those perceptions is strengthened by feedback from a cross section of employees who interface regularly with the individual and come to similar conclusions. Look for the development themes mentioned by two or more. Ignore the outlier comment from just one team member. Perceptions help establish the developmental agenda for each employee. They provide anecdotal examples of what may show up as developmental recommendations in a variety of assessment tools.

» Does development develop? Yes, typically, but not always in the same way for everyone! The development agenda is unique to each box on the New Nine Box Grid, and it is dynamic within a healthy organizational culture where every team member has absolute clarity on the mission, vision, and values. Whatever is needed to move each team member toward the upper right area of the grid is part of their agenda for further development.

» The New Nine Box Grid provides a tool to assess the performance, potential, and personal drive of each supervisor, manager, and leader. The intention is to move them to the upper right section of the grid, which implies hardwiring to enhance new competencies and behaviors. Without a development plan resulting from that annual assessment, the natural tendency is to slip further away from the upper right. Without a plan, learning is not always applied. Without application, new habits are not hardwired.

If you don't know the uniqueness

of each direct report,

then you will never understand

how to uniquely develop

them either.

HARDWIRE CONNECTION #4

IT ALL HAPPENS ON THREE LEVELS

Is there an organizational structure that fosters development?

HARDWIRE CONNECTION #4—
IT ALL HAPPENS ON THREE LEVELS

IS THERE AN ORGANIZATIONAL
STRUCTURE THAT
FOSTERS DEVELOPMENT?

ONCE WE IDENTIFIED PATHWAYS to growth-oriented learning and clearly articulated the mission, vision, and values of leadership development, then we were able to focus on the individuals who are on the journey to enhance their leadership capacity. What does it take to hardwire their new leadership habits? Three levels of connection must intersect and engage together or hardwiring will be short circuited. In Hardwire Connection #4, we determined that we needed to distinguish among the organizational, the team, and the individual levels.

The Organizational Level: Leading the Enterprise

Leading at the organizational, system, or enterprise level will require the highest level of leadership responsibility with a greater emphasis on strategy than on operational tactics. This level of leading involves a unique mixture of leadership competencies that differ from leading at the team or individual level. Yes, there are core leadership competencies needed for every supervisor, manager, and leader, but executive leadership is at a higher level of organizational complexity and responsibility, and therefore, at a higher level of accountability.

Since leadership competencies are most often learned competencies, C-Suite leaders and their executive direct reports need continuing development in the areas unique to their leadership roles and skills. The manager and supervisor roles follow in addressing their own professional development in areas relevant to mid-level positions.

This trilogy of roles for supervisors, managers, and leaders within GOR Inc. define, shape, model, expect, and reward our commitment to developing teams and team members. It's where hardwiring new leadership habits continues. It takes an organization-wide commitment to create a culture of development for team members at every level of employment. It starts as a trickle-down process and eventually becomes a trickle-up process throughout the entire company.

When we started our analysis in Hardwire Connection #4, we couldn't ignore our culture. Since development occurs within a company's culture, we felt it was essential to define the uniqueness of the GOR Inc. culture. What does it include? What are our dysfunctions? What's missing? As the findings were shared within our subgroup for review and discussion, our questions and brainstorming time led us to recognize the need for a baseline of understanding by completing a culture diagnosis. We were guilty of conscious incompetence. We were aware that we didn't know what we needed to know.

We did understand that whatever our culture is, it is like the computer operating system that always runs in the background during our attempts to build the developmental value for every employee. We needed to find out if our operating system was facilitating or inhibiting the development of every employee as well as the hardwiring of their new leadership habits. We storyboarded the essential elements. Out of our conversation, we created our own culture diagnostic tool for a comprehensive overview. We simply call it...

Ten Culture Questions

1. Are the mission, vision, values, and strategy clear and consistently communicated to everyone?

2. How prevalent are political minefields that must be navigated and negotiated to compete for limited resources?

3. What are the spoken and unspoken rules, and does anyone get a pass?

4. Are there personalities who set the positive or negative mood for everyone else. Do we tolerate the negative, and if so, why?

5. Are there intentional team-building activities that enhance camaraderie and contribute to trust?

6. Is the company a collection of silos, or do teams and team members get to work collaboratively across typical workplace boundaries?

7. How is conflict perceived and managed?

8. How is failure addressed and success celebrated?

9. Are people micromanaged or given full responsibility and authority to execute on delegated assignments? In other words, how is authority exerted?

10. How is work-life balance modeled and encouraged? How is it handled when an employee is experiencing a great imbalance in this area?

Our subgroup wrestled for a long time with two ideas embedded in the ten questions: Which of the ten is the most troubling, and which is the most critical in closing the gap between the ideal in our mission and vision statements compared to the reality of our daily work life.

We built consensus around a Fourth Wall idea: Leaders are the curators of organizational culture. A curator is defined as "keeper or custodian of a museum or other collection,"[1] so it seemed like a fitting word to use. We borrowed and reapplied the concept for our purposes in this Fourth Wall project. In a business environment, curators are the keepers of organizational culture. In turn, culture is a collection of the mission, vision, and values.

We rarely get to leave ideas in the theoretical realm in our discussions at work. Suzanne is the gold standard for a CEO who is a curator of our organizational culture! The question that we all know she would eventually ask is: "What does that mean in how we lead our teams?" We articulated the following framework...

Seven Responsibilities of Curating Leaders

1. **Declare Your Culture.** Announce the mission, vision, and values that define the ideal.

2. **Define Your Values.** Values are not ideas to believe but behaviors to live. The greater the clarity, the less confusion in understanding and application.

3. **Illustrate the Behaviors.** Create a word picture of what each value looks like when applied to our daily interactions with other team members, vendors, customers, and even our competition.

4. **Model the Behaviors.** The consistency of our attitudes, words, and behaviors will reinforce our commitment to everyone else and to our culture.

5. **Expect the Behaviors.** Include the culture story as part of onboarding at every level of employment.

6. **Measure the Accountability.** Provide immediate feedback when the ideal/real gap widens for any team member.

7. **Reward the Success.** Celebrate the examples of when the culture story represents the heart of your corporate identity.

The commitment we are making at the organizational level is that every supervisor, manager, and leader is expected to be a curating leader who prioritizes the value of developing every employee on their team. Yes, we have other organizational values, but we were spotlighting the development value in order to justify and make the case for our ongoing budgetary expenditures in order to make it happen. To operationalize this, we established "Developmental Service Standards" that we call...

Four Guardrails

» **Inclusiveness**—It's ideally giving every employee an opportunity for development, either to do their current role more effectively and more efficiently or to begin to prepare them for the next role further up in the company hierarchy..

» **Clarity**—Articulating the core behaviors and/or the core competencies that are needed and may vary at each employment category.

» **Logistics**—The practical questions of the where, when, and how of providing development opportunities and the resources needed for success.

» **Inspiration**—Casting vision to help the individual see their potential and also their impact on the productivity of the team and the entire organization.

Without ownership and buy-in by every supervisor, manager, and leader, modeling this value and demonstrating a consistent expectation, an organization is stymied in achieving its developmental mission and vision. When all categories of leaders commit to their own professional development, it enhances their leadership capacity and models professional growth and development to each of their direct reports.

As a result, the productive potential of each team member, and the team itself, increases. Individuals make up teams and teams make up the organization. The organization's cultural value of professional development flows from the organization to the team to the individual (trickle down), and from the individual to the team to the organization (trickle up). That's the dynamic nature of a developmental culture.

The Team Level: Leading Others

Leading and managing are two different assignments. Both leaders and managers lead and manage. Leaders invest the majority of their attention on strategy (leadership) and less on operations (management). At the same time, managers do lead strategically but most of their energy, time, and attention are given to managing the tactical operations.

In simplistic terms, managers focus on mission and leaders focus on vision. Author, James Grady writes, "As Peter Drucker once proclaimed, management is doing things right—improving operational performance, maximizing revenues, and reducing expenses while increasing artistic production values and audience appreciation. Leadership is doing the right things—setting organizational priorities and allocating human and fiscal resources to fulfill the organization's vision."[2]

Alongside leaders and managers, we are recognizing the more tactical role of the supervisors as well. They complete the way in which companies oversee the work of employees at all levels of the organization. In summary, we can say that leaders lead, managers manage, and supervisors supervise. All three need development opportunities to improve their effectiveness in accomplishing strategic goals with their teams. What does it take at the team level for leaders, managers, and supervisors to shape a culture that contributes to the development of each employee? What does it take to hardwire their new leadership habits? We identified four non-negotiables.

» The Leader/Manager/Supervisor Invests in the Individual
They must first be equipped for intentional and ongoing professional development conversations with each direct report. In doing so, they should make it a priority to advocate for each employee's professional development in such a way that they feel supported. Good leaders do this in spite of the realization that some might eventually move on to other opportunities within the company or elsewhere. It's simply a risk worth taking.

Search Institute's model of community development provides an answer of how this can happen in any organization. They have been focused on developing healthy communities in a counterintuitive way. Rather than identify the issues and then seek ways to fix those problems, they propose building on a community's strengths. Search Institute's research has created The Developmental Assets® Framework which identifies "40 positive supports and strengths that young people need to succeed. Half of the assets focus on relationships and opportunities they need in their families, schools, and communities (external assets). The remaining assets focus on the social-emotional strengths, values, and commitments that are nurtured within young people (internal assets)."[3]

While Search Institute's research focuses on young people, their insight is valuable to organizations seeking to create a development culture. One of the 40 Assets identified is the prevalence of developmental relationships. When leaders see their role as the leader-coach with each direct report, it contributes to the collective and collaborative health of the entire company. It's the trickle-down strategy in action! What does that mean for supervisors, managers, and leaders? The Search Institute model includes five elements and twenty actions of developmental relationships:

1. Express Care. Show me that I matter to you.
    Actions: Be dependable, listen, believe in me, be warm, and encourage.

2. Challenge Growth. Push me to keep getting better.
    Actions: Expect my best, stretch me, hold me accountable, and reflect on my failures.

3. Provide Support. Help me complete my tasks and achieve goals.
    Actions: Navigate, empower, advocate, and set boundaries.

4. Share Power. Treat me with respect and give me a say.
    Actions: Respect me, include me, collaborate, and let me lead.

5. Expand Possibilities. Connect me with people and places that broaden my world.
    Actions: Inspire, broaden my horizons, and connect.

If supervisors, managers, and leaders invest in each team member in these five ways, it operationalizes the value of development. Not only that, but it creates a point of contact for communication, support, and accountability throughout the entire company.

» The Leader/Manager/Supervisor coaches Each Team Member Differently

Leaders who invest in developmental relationships have discovered the difference between building a team and building up a team. Building a team requires us to operate on the task side of the workplace continuum. Building up a team requires us to focus in a balanced way on the people as well as on the tasks. Leaders who know best will seek to acknowledge the great contributions made by those on the task-oriented side of the continuum, and they will challenge those who err on the people side while missing task expectations.

THE PEOPLE — TASK GRAPH

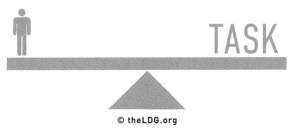

© theLDG.org

As we saw in Hardwire Connection #3, members of one's team can be scattered across the Nine Box Grid. Each one is also at a different point on the "People—Task Continuum." Leaders and managers have the responsibility of meeting each direct report at their point of need, whether it's more encouragement or a greater degree of challenge in their work or professional development. Ella Wheeler Wilcox, an American poet and journalist, said it well: "A pat on the back is only a few vertebrae removed from a kick in the pants..."[4] The goal of either is to motivate someone toward their full potential. When you find the right fulcrum point on that continuum for each team member, then you move them toward the upper right corner on the New Nine Box Grid where they will be more effective in their current role.

» **The Leader/Manager/Supervisor Asks More Than Tells**
Questions are the most powerful tool in one's leadership toolbox. It's not always having the right answer. Sometimes your best leadership action is asking the right question as a means of checking in and bringing accountability for each of your direct reports and their current assignments. It's also a subtle way to begin to address their career development conversations. How you ask and how you listen is key. Learn to ask and then pause in silence for their answer. The pause is always awkward for the team member as they gather their thoughts to answer your question. Not everyone finds these conversations easy, but everyone deserves a chance to grow.

Our project subgroup identified a few prompts to use in opening those informal conversations wherever they occur. You can use these, or your own questions, to bring accountability but also to establish conversational ways of relating to each direct report in a developmental way. These prompts will set the stage to more intentional career growth conversations as well.

» The Obvious Question—Do you need my help?

» The Inquisitive Question—What do I need to know from you today?

» The Awkward Question—How are you keeping me from being blindsided in your work on this project?

» The Benchmark Question—What's your plan to keep me informed at the key decision points in the completion of this project?

» The Mistake Question—What are the insights you have gained from the mistake made that will strengthen your work going forward?

» The Development Question—What skills or resources were needed to complete this project that we did not realize at the beginning?

» The Completion Question—How can I best recognize your accomplishment to celebrate a job well done?

Accountability is that delicate balance between what's too much and what's not enough? Your answer will vary with each team member. The more you are interacting with them, the more you will learn how best to maintain the right balance of accountability for each one. The leadership assignment is that you also move from accountability to advocacy in their continuing development. It's one of the best ways you can show you care!

» The Leader/Manager/Supervisor Initiates Career Conversations

Every supervisor, manager, or leader is equipped and expected to have ongoing career conversations with each direct report. It's not complicated, but it shouldn't just be tacked on at the end of their annual review...if there is time. The Society for Human Resource Management (SHRM) has developed a simple format called the "Stay Interview."[5] Their material offers insight in how to set up the interview as well as the questions to ask about a direct report's career plans and development needs to achieve them. They use the term "Stay Interview" because this commitment to develop team members and hardwire new leadership habits contributes to the retention of team members who are finding both career growth opportunities and personal support in the company where they currently work.

Stay conversations can be part of a company's strategy to engage their best talent. It is a structured way to talk with your direct reports about the next steps in their career planning that will contribute to greater job satisfaction. The conversations are not lengthy, but leaders must schedule a one-on-one just for this purpose rather than adding it on to the end of a different agenda. Ask about what they need and want from their work. Ask about their career aspirations: "What are your short-term and long-term professional goals?" You may be surprised that some are not thinking about where their career is headed or how to get there.

Many people are afraid to express their long-term career dreams or plans to their boss as that might be perceived to be discontent in their current role and reporting relationship. Others think they could take over as CEO tomorrow and will not hesitate to let you know. There is such a wide range of personalities, and that is what makes our job so vital. We need to meet people where they are at, help them be the most effective in their current role, encourage them to set appropriate professional goals, and do our part to coach them toward achieving those goals. Provide time for conversation and planning about what will be needed for their next steps to prepare them for promotion into responsibilities with greater complexity. Offer to support them in what will be needed. Make it acceptable and expected that they are on a development pathway to enhance their productive potential whether they stay or leave for an opportunity elsewhere, even if it's to work for your competitor! If you find that you are fearful of losing people to the competition, then you are likely inhibiting growth within your organization.

Supporting our team members at GOR Inc. in their career goals is a tangible way our company operationalizes the mission, vision, and values of a development culture. Doing so moves us from an organizational value of what we believe to implementation of that belief within each team. That eventually trickles down to every individual. Growth is expected. It's expected of everyone. This communicates an attitude of interest and support with a message that says, "You matter to our company." Stay interviews give employees a reason to stay. After living through "the great resignation" during the prolonged shutdown caused by the COVID-19 pandemic, we all know that retention of our best leaders is critical. Stay interviews just might help you perform fewer exit interviews!

The Individual Level: Leading Yourself

In order to supervise others, we must first supervise ourselves. In order to manage others, we must first manage ourselves. In order to lead others, we must first work on leading ourselves. Almost no one talks about this, yet it is an important component of professional development and growth. If we are committed to a development culture in our organization, and we are committed to developing our team, we must be invested in our own continuing development as well. It's not just about modeling this behavior, it's about the continual drive for improvement that makes us better leaders and better human beings. As mentioned in the opening to a fantastic article on Inc.com, Bill Green mentioned the role of the founder in building a good company culture. He referred to Lee Iococa, the great American automobile executive who said, "the speed of the boss is the speed of the team."[6] If you are not on a development pathway, then don't expect your team to do what you are not yet doing.

» The Individual is the Owner

What does it take at the individual level to hardwire new leadership habits? It begins with personal ownership of the responsibility to chart your own progress and development, acknowledging that no one else will do it for you. You are writing a story. You are writing *your* story. There are always factors that impact the story, but it's still your own story. When you hit a dead end that someone or something else prompted, it's still up to you to find a way around the obstacle. Rather than think of it as a dead end, visualize it as a toll booth on the highway. Yes, you are stopped, but when you pay the toll, you may continue on toward your next career development destination.

What story do you want to tell? What story are you trying to tell? Is it your story or the story someone else tried to impose on you? Every choice or decision is part of your story. Sure, there are parts of it we'd like to forget or relive differently. Rather than focus on regrets, we need to take advantage of learning opportunities that lead to new skills and a new future in spite of any negatives from our past. Start a journey that you are excited to live because it represents you at your best!

Personal ownership is demonstrated in one's personal drive. It's what distinguishes some employees who want to excel from other employees who are content to settle. At the individual level, it's the supervisor, manager, or leader who is motivated to not only learn, but also to apply the learning that it takes to accomplish three things:

1. To push themself toward achieving and experiencing their productive potential.

2. To step into new stretch assignments, applying new learning that propels them toward career advancement.

3. To increase their value to their team and the entire organization by leading more effectively and efficiently.

If you don't own your need for development, no one else will do it for you. Hardwiring is impossible without ownership and personal responsibility for the areas of leadership that need further work.

» The Individual is the Transparent

The best way to grow is to find out what you don't yet know about yourself. It's a two-way street. You have to give people feedback about yourself, and you have to ask people for their feedback about you. Joe Luft and Harry Ingram's famous Johari Window model gives insight into your self-perceptions and the perceptions of other people.[7]

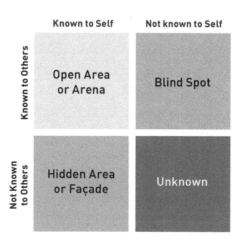

The Johari Window Model

The Open Area—Information about your attitudes, behavior, emotions, habits, mannerisms, feelings, skills, and views will be known by other people as well as by yourself. The goal is not to have a large open area with everyone, but rather with your most trusted connections. There is strength and benefit to living with a large open area with a few people who know you and will offer both their unconditional acceptance as well as their honest and constructive feedback.

The Hidden Area—This is information known to you but not to others. It includes past events, experiences, fears, secrets, mistakes, and failures. We keep this information to ourselves because we are not sure what others would think of us if they knew, and we fear what others might do with the information.

The Unknown Area—This is information we are not aware of, nor are others, related to our interests, strengths, capabilities, and talents. We may not yet have training or experience to introduce us to certain things, and it's important to recognize that. Expanding our networks can lead to new insights and new opportunities in areas we have interest and/or aptitude.

The Blind Spot This is information about yourself that others observe but you are unaware of. This includes mannerisms, habits, words overused or used incorrectly, a lack of emotional and social intelligence, biases, offensive behaviors, and political incorrectness. Blind spots can complicate interpersonal relationships as people hesitate to give honest feedback.

The four panes of the window are never actually equal in size; that is never the goal. If you want to develop your skills as a supervisor, manager, or leader, then enlarge the size of the Open Area by reducing the sizes of the Hidden Area and Blind Spot. You do this by giving a few trusted people honest feedback about who you are. It also requires you to be vulnerable and ask for feedback on what they perceive about you. Their perception is their reality of who you are and will give you clues about what you need to work on within your leadership development agenda. Ask four simple questions from a few who know you best:

1. What am I really good at that I should keep doing?

2. What am I good at that I need to get better at because it's so critical to my role?

3. What is in my blind spot that gets in the way of my effectiveness that I should stop doing?

4. What best practices of leading am I not yet practicing that I need to start doing?

Without the courage to be vulnerable, you will never ask, and no one will ever tell. Without vulnerability, you won't own the responsibility for your professional development. If you don't own it, you'll miss hardwiring the habits that make you a better leader. When you lose, your team loses, and the organization loses too, but it's a triple win when you ask, tell, listen, and grow!

» The Individual is Focused on the Few

What does it take at the individual level to hardwire new leadership habits? The third idea in our consideration of the individual is to have a manageable focus. Admit you have a challenge, but the things you can do to mature in your leadership are sometimes too numerous.

Maintaining a manageable focus implies that you have limited resources of time and the capability to do what is required. Focus is not concentration. You can pay too much attention to the wrong details, but there is power when you focus on the most important thing. It keeps you from being distracted by other urgent matters.

When we think of "focus," we think of "distinctness" and "clarity." Distinctness means you are only addressing the top few growth areas on your master list at any given time. Whatever else is on your list is for another day. Clarity means that you refine, with specificity, exactly what you need to address in your top few growth areas. Focus is freeing. Focus allows you to declare leadership development success rather than feeling guilty because you didn't tackle the entire list of developmental recommendations.

Staying focused does not give you permission to ignore urgent matters. Imagine a dart board:

What are two or three leadership habits that you need to strengthen or develop? That's the bullseye on your target. Everything else is secondary in your professional growth agenda and lands on one of the outer rings. Focus requires that you spend the majority of your development time on the bullseye items. The urgent things that show up daily need to be managed or delegated to others.

What specific areas of professional growth will make the difference for you in your current role? What specific things do you want to be equipped to do as you look forward to a future role? Focus on the few and you will see results!

Final Thoughts

The organization, the team, and the individual all work together to reinforce the sustainability of new leadership habits in each employee. Developmental organizations operationalize the value of creating a growth culture for every employee.

» The organization builds a developmental culture at every level of employment by training team leaders to coach, support, and encourage the development of each direct report through regular career conversations.

» The team leader advocates as the "leader-coach" in paying attention to operationalizing the cultural value of development for each direct report.

» The individual displays personal drive to take advantage of new learning while finding incremental ways to apply learning to new leadership habits.

When you pay attention to the individual level by leading yourself, then you are ready to contribute to the team level by leading others. If you master the team level, then you are ready to consider the organizational level of leading the entire enterprise. That is the "trickle up" sequence from the individual to the team to the organization.

The ultimate question to ask every team member at each level is: How high can you lead? It's the capacity question. Are you ready and equipped with the skills needed to lead at a higher level of organizational responsibility? Every time you invest in developing more effective and more efficient leadership habits, it expands and enhances your leadership capacity.

FOURTH WALL CONCLUSION

Developmental organizations make developmental teams possible. Developmental teams make developing individuals possible. When all three intersect and work together toward the same mission, vision, and values, then the probability of hardwiring new leadership habits increases.

The organization is critical.

The team is essential.

The individual is non-negotiable.

People can't achieve individual progress without the team leader encouraging and supporting each of their direct reports. Team leaders can't effectively lead the way for the development of each direct report if the organization doesn't value a development culture. Organizations aren't really committed to the value of development unless they invest, with the right mindset and real dollars, in what is needed to make that value a reality for every employee at every level of the organization.

Leadership Development

on Three Levels

...Team members can't achieve

professional development without

the team leader's encouragement

and support.

...Supervisors, managers, and leaders

can't develop team members

if the organization doesn't value

a development culture.

...Organizations can't live out the value

of development unless it invests

in the resources needed at every

level of employment.

HARDWIRE CONNECTION #5

WHEN LEARNING IS APPLIED

How does an individual translate learning into new leadership habits?

» Something's Missing

» Seven Rules of Reflection

» Final Thoughts

» Fourth Wall Conclusion

HARDWIRE CONNECTION #5—
WHEN LEARNING IS APPLIED

HOW DOES AN INDIVIDUAL
TRANSLATE LEARNING INTO
NEW LEADERSHIP HABITS?

THE CENTER FOR CREATIVE LEADERSHIP (CCL) has been doing research into the development of leaders for decades. Their 70-20-10 rule, developed after thirty years of research, is based on the premise that "leadership can be learned" and asserts how that leader invests their time to develop specific competencies or behaviors is very important. In our terminology at GOR Inc. we suggest a sequence of steps in the learning process: Content Identification, Social Interaction, and Experiential Application.[1]

Michael Lombardo and Robert Eichinger at the Center for Creative Leadership conducted a survey of 200 executives to self-report how they believed they learned and applied that learning:

10% is content—introduced in a variety of ways (reading, webinar, podcast, etc.).

20% is social—talking with a colleague or coach about how that learning applies.

70% is experiential—applying that learning in challenging assignments as an incremental test of change.[2]

In Hardwire Connection #5, our team applied the 70-20-10 approach and our interpretation of the research applied to our unique situation. Among other things, we created this formula:

Micro Learning + Macro Application = Incremental Change

Lombardo and Eichinger, in the same book that was cited earlier, indicated the rationale of this model of learning and application: "Development generally begins with a realization of current or future need and the motivation to do something about it. This might come from feedback, a mistake, watching other people's reactions, failing, or not being up to a task—in other words, from experience. The odds are that development will be about 70% from on-the-job experiences—working on tasks and problems; about 20% from feedback and observing good and bad examples of the need; and 10% from courses and reading."

Something's Missing

It's a counterintuitive approach that minimizes the amount of learning and emphasizes the application of how that learning leads to new leadership habits. In our work in Hardwire Connection #5, the linear flow from learning to discussion of the learning to application makes intuitive sense of how we work toward new sustainable habits. It's not new leadership work, or even more work, but doing the work you are already doing and doing it differently.

In our approach to strengthening the business case for hardwiring new habits, we concluded that we wanted to see a fourth component added to the model that is essential to the sustainability of hardwiring new leadership habits. We called it: Reflection Following Application.

At GOR Inc., we considered a slightly different model that includes this fourth component: Think, Talk, Act, Reflect. This model of development was created by The Leadership Development Group in 2008 and led to our idea of Reflection Following Application. Here is the overview:

> **...Think.** The first step in development is to understand what you need to know about a specific leadership behavior or competency in order to understand its significance and application in your current or anticipated leadership role? How is someone described who is skilled in this area? How about someone who is unskilled? The counterintuitive aspect of this model reminds us that we don't have to learn a lot to develop further as a leader. New habits can be very specific areas of behavior or skills that are not complicated to understand but tricky to implement. Learning is incremental and so is development.

> **...Talk.** Discuss the micro learning and the macro application connected to the leader's unique situation. This could be conversations with a colleague, leadership coach, or participation in a professional learning community inside or outside your company. The conversations expand your understanding of the information and invite you to internalize the value of application. A coach could help you explore scenarios that are customized to your workplace reality.

...Act. Application is what transforms when you build new habits. These are the stretch assignments that are not new work, or more work, but doing the work you are already doing in new and incrementally better ways. Trial and error are part of learning new attitudes, words, and behaviors that demonstrate positive influence in your character and effective action in your competence as a growing leader.

...Reflect. Reviewing what you've learned and how you've started applying it should be a somewhat structured process. It leads to another cycle of learning, valuing, applying, and reviewing in incremental steps for each iteration of personal growth and development. Reflection is the often missing ingredient needed to reinforce the application of learning and hardwiring the new leadership habits identified in that learning.

Seven Rules of Self-Reflection

Self-reflection leads to self-awareness. Self-awareness is essential in admitting that there is room for personal growth and development in critical leadership behaviors and competencies. You will never admit your need for new leadership habits to others if you are unable to admit it to yourself. Looking in the mirror necessitates following the Seven Rules of Self-Reflection:

1. **Time.** When will you stop and review your application, your progress, your missteps, and your successes?

2. **Start Small.** Incremental is the key idea. You might only work on one specific leadership skill. At the most, do no more than four.

3. **Hold Yourself Accountable.** No one can or will do it for you.

4. **Check Your Feelings.** How challenging was it to do things differently? How hard was the change? How hard was the consistency of application? Of the five basic emotions, which one(s) did you experience: mad, sad, glad, afraid, ashamed?

5. **Observe Others.** Are there leaders inside or outside your company who model the skill you are working on? Ask for their insights.

6. **Ask for Feedback.** Does anyone know you are working on this aspect of your leadership skills? Did anyone notice and tell you their observations? Who can you ask?

7. **Be Forgiving.** We are looking for incremental steps of growth. No one is ever perfect in the first steps of seeking personal change.

Final Thoughts

Reflection is both personal and interpersonal. Alongside self-reflection, select a group of work associates to provide a reality check on your potentially biased self-observations. This stakeholder group will give ongoing feedback in real time as you hardwire new habits in your portfolio of leadership skills. These are the "asking and telling" relationships reflected in the Johari Window. It takes courage to be vulnerable and invite selected and trusted colleagues to hold you accountable. It's how you make ongoing adjustments in applying new learning which leads to new habits. It's a process, and the application may not be quite perfect at first. Whatever we eventually do well, chances are, we did it poorly at first.

FOURTH WALL CONCLUSION

Micro learning from a variety of sources lends itself to macro application of new leadership insights. Self-reflection is a deliberate, honest, and objective review of your thoughts, feelings, emotions, and changes in your existing leadership habits. Feedback from a trusted group of colleagues corrects your personal bias and refines your clarity on what to apply and how to apply it. Even the smallest incremental change compounded over time can contribute to new habitual ways of leading. Our review and discussion of the insights in Hardwire Connection #5 challenged our investment in leadership development resources. We all agree that learning without application is a waste of organizational resources. When application develops new habitual ways of leading that are hardwired, then leadership effectiveness and efficiency improve and organizational performance is enhanced.

Learning enlarges your

view of who you have

not yet become.

Applied learning expands

who you already are.

HARDWIRE CONNECTION #6

CONNECTING THREE WIRES

*What is needed to strengthen the hardwiring
of new leadership habits?*

» Coaching—Professional Accountability

» Feedback—Team Accountability

» Reflection—Personal Accountability

» Final Thoughts

» Fourth Wall Conclusion

HARDWIRE CONNECTION #6— CONNECTING THREE WIRES

WHAT IS NEEDED TO
STRENGTHEN THE HARDWIRING
OF NEW LEADERSHIP HABITS?

BOB PROCTOR'S COMMENT has guided our thinking: "Accountability is the glue that ties commitment to the result."[1] Our stereotypical and unsuccessful New Year's resolutions are reminders of the challenge of learning, committing, applying, and hardwiring new habits. The Association for Talent Development (ATD) did a study on accountability which was summarized by Stephen Newland of the Association for Financial Counseling & Planning Education®. The researchers at ATD found that individuals have an increasing probability of completing a goal by doing the following:

10% likely to "complete a goal by having an idea or a goal."

25% likely by "consciously deciding that you will do it."

40% likely by "deciding when you will do it."

50% likely by "planning how to do it."

65% likely by "committing to someone that you will do it."

95% likely by "having a specific accountability appointment with someone you've committed to."[2]

In Hardwire Connection #6, our "hardwiring" metaphor is illustrated in the idea of connecting three wires. Each wire represents a different dimension of accountability:

> 1. Professional accountability through leadership coaching
>
> 2. Team accountability through stakeholder feedback
>
> 3. Personal accountability through objective reflection

Doing all three increases the probability of getting to the 65 percent likelihood of hardwiring new habits.

> » The coach is the external voice.
>
> » The team is the organizational voice.
>
> » The individual is that internal voice.

The pressing question from any one of these three sources is simply: Are you intentionally moving from your commitment of applying new learning to actually developing new habitual ways of leading?

Coaching—Professional Accountability

The Institute of Coaching, connected to Harvard Medical School, cites that "80% of people who receive coaching report increased self-confidence, and over 70% of individuals who receive coaching benefited from improved work performance, relationships, and more effective communication skills. 86% of companies feel that they recouped the investment they made into coaching plus more on top."[3] The results of coaching are impacted by the length of the coaching engagement.

Brandon Mergard at Stakeholder Centered Coaching completed his master's degree research at Aston University in 2019 on "The Role of Time in Executive Coaching Effectiveness: a longitudinal analysis of perceived changes in leadership effectiveness."[4] The study involved 500+ responses across three time horizons, assessing perceived changes in leadership effectiveness (PCLE) evaluated by critical stakeholders of senior executives operating primarily in Fortune500 organizations on 4 continents. Each executive had an executive coach, selected 1-2 behavioral growth areas, and captured changes in PCLE at 6, 9, and 12 months of coaching. The findings aimed to inform suppliers, purchasers, and consumers of executive coaching by providing insight towards the optimal duration of a coaching engagement.

Mergard's aim was to explore time as a "key ingredient" in successful engagements with the intent of capitalizing on the unique and competitive advantage of Stakeholder Centered Coaching®. The research question was: "What is the effect of time on perceived changes in leadership effectiveness" as it relates to executive coaching. Mergard's dataset of 580 responses revealed 100 percent of leaders being coached using the Stakeholder Centered Coaching® methodology were recognized and acknowledged by key stakeholders within six months. Additionally, and perhaps most importantly, were the significant changes across each time spectrum. Using Goldsmith and Morgan's tool for measuring perceived changes in leadership effectiveness, the minimum score after twelve months of coaching was 70.67 percent higher than at six months of coaching.

The findings shed new light on the potential role of time in executive coaching and suggests a twelve-month engagement may be more beneficial for leaders and their stakeholders than a shorter duration. The study addresses the enhanced change of perception by each stakeholder after a longer coaching engagement with the Stakeholder Centered Coaching® methodology. We are extrapolating the idea that the change in perception of the leader is the result of improved leadership habits that are perceived by key stakeholders over time.

In our review of Mergard's research, we are concluding that coaching engagements should be extended beyond a typical six-month engagement to reinforce the sustainability of new leadership habits. The extended time brings continuing accountability and feedback to strengthen the hardwiring of those new leadership skills. Coaching does reinforce the application of new learning by managing, monitoring, and measuring progress on the road to hardwiring new habits.

In our work on Hardwire Connection #6, we acknowledge that we have always included two tools to support the value of a longer coaching engagement by providing more objective insight into the leadership behaviors and leadership competencies needing attention:

> ...**Coaching Tool #1**—360-degree interviews (360s) are time intensive if done through personal interviews rather than an online process. Interviews by phone or virtual video technology provide the nuanced interaction with direct reports, peers, and senior leaders or board members to explore their perceptions of the individual being coached. Typically, 360s include three direct reports, three peers, and three senior leaders or board members. Themes emerge from the questions asked that contribute to a master list of potential focus areas for coaching.

...**Coaching Tool #2**—Research-based assessments add insight into what competencies or behaviors are considered as potential focus areas for coaching. Our team chose to use the Hogan Leadership Forecast Assessment series to review Personality, Development, and Motives/Values/Preferences.[5] Hogan's assessments are more about reputation than they are about identity. Each assessment illustrates the gap between self-perception and that of others on specific scales. In some ways the 360-degree interviews identify themes that are anecdotal illustrations of many findings in the Hogan assessments. Each assessment report provides sections of Developmental Recommendations that guide the coach and the leader in prioritizing the top few areas that will make the greatest contribution to leading more effectively and efficiently. There are many good performance assessments out there, this is simply one of the best.

Feedback—Team Accountability

Feedback from a select group of work associates can provide any leader with real-time insights into their development progress as well as their prioritized next steps. Those closest to the leader on a daily working basis can provide perceptive and insightful feedback throughout the coaching engagement. What is observable to your co-workers every day can be summarized in three ideas: attitudes, words, and behaviors. Attitudes lead to words. Words lead to behaviors. Learning influences all three. It sounds very linear and sequential, but as you know, it's much more dynamic in our work and personal life! Many of us on this journey can say:

> » New *learning* informs how I define the reality of life, work, and people in different ways than I have up to this point in time.

» That informed reality shapes my *attitudes* toward the organization, those I lead, as well as those I follow.

» New attitudes get translated into *words* I use to talk about my leadership practice.

» New words describe the *behaviors* that test out new potential habits in how I lead.

Here is an individual's thinking process: "I am learning new insights about leadership, and I am thinking about those insights to understand them more thoroughly. I am talking with others about how they apply, and I am beginning to use them in my daily practice. It's not new work or more work but just leading differently. How I am being perceived by co-workers is demonstrated in my attitudes, words, and behaviors. My openness to their feedback is a sign of my ongoing willingness to be accountable for my professional development."

Two tools provide a means of strengthening accountability to your team:

...**Team Feedback Tool #1**—The Check-In Survey. The Marshall Goldsmith team at Stakeholder Centered Coaching provides a simple tool to facilitate regular feedback or as they call it, Feedforward.[6] Here is a sample of a check-in survey, developed with the concepts from the Marshall Goldsmith team and customized by The Leadership Development Group. It only takes a few minutes to complete. It's based on a seven-point scale. The range goes from someone getting worse (-1, -2, or -3) to someone getting better (+1, +2, 0r +3) and indicates improvement in specific areas of coaching. Zero indicates no change.

-3 -2 -1 0 +1 +2 +3

The survey provides real time feedback from stakeholders regarding their perceptions of the leader. Stakeholders are aware that the leader is working on a few professional development areas to become a better supervisor, manager, or leader. The Check-In Survey is done at the mid-point of coaching and then at the end of coaching. The survey is a way to capture feedback/feedforward that helps leaders adjust their application of learning in order to hardwire the best of their new leadership habits. The following illustration provides a sample of the Check-In Survey.

Leadership is a learned competency

Some leaders are born leaders.
Most leaders are made leaders.

✔ Coaching helps identify the competencies needing further development.

✔ Micro-learning increases one's understanding in order to apply new ideas.

✔ New skills lead to incremental change in one's habits of leading.

✔ Feedback and reflection guide your next iteration of learning and application.

Leadership Development Check-In Survey

Thank you for your availability to provide insights that contribute to our development of leaders. Your input will be valuable in the next phase of the leadership coaching for (name). There are four numerical questions on the survey asking for your reflection on (name's) work in specific focus areas we have addressed in coaching sessions, and then two open-ended questions are provided for your comments. Your reply will be confidential as your answers will be collated with others for an overall summary. Please send me an email with your four numbers and your responses to the two questions. I am a raving fan of your company's investment in developing its leaders at all levels. Thank you for your time in replying!

The Leadership Development Group
www.theLDG.org

1. **Coaching focus area #1: Be less critical of people and processes.**

-3	-2	-1	0	+1	+2	+3
Less Effective			No Change			More Effective

2. **Coaching focus area #2: Empower employees to do more operations work through delegation.**

-3	-2	-1	0	+1	+2	+3
Less Effective			No Change			More Effective

3. **Coaching focus area #3: Focus more on strategic leadership and less on tactical operations.**

-3	-2	-1	0	+1	+2	+3
Less Effective			No Change			More Effective

4. **How would you rate changes in _____'s overall leadership effectiveness?**

-3	-2	-1	0	+1	+2	+3
Less Effective			No Change			More Effective

5. **What has _____ done in leading in recent months that you have found particularly effective?**

6. **What one thing would you like _____ to do differently moving forward?**

...Team Feedback Tool #2—Emotional Intelligence (EQ). It's letting the thinking side of the brain catch up to the feeling side of the brain in response to people or situations that trigger an emotional response. EQ includes four elements: (1) an awareness of what triggers your emotional response, (2) an awareness of what emotion you are feeling at any point in time, (3) an awareness of the level of intensity of the emotion you are feeling, and (4). the management of how, when, where, to whom, and if you express the emotion.

Emotions are the interpersonal currency that either reinforce best practice leadership habits or ruin the best intentions. *Green, Yellow, Red* can be a useful tool for EQ growth to help monitor the emotional tone of a team discussion or a one-on-one meeting. Think of it as a team traffic light!

» **Green** means all is well. Let's keep moving forward. Any conflict is between ideas and not taken personally in any way. Emotions remain low and are managed easily.

» **Yellow** means that we are proceeding with caution. We should be aware of our need to be thoughtful when discussing competing ideas and our emotional investment in the idea we are advocating.

» **Red** means we all know this is not going well and stopping is a must. Conflict is escalating between personalities and emotions are growing in their intensity. Resentment and unresolved conflict are possible.

This simple team tool allows any team member to ask, "Where are we just now, and how is this going for us so far?" They are acknowledging that it may be the wrong time for the right conversation or the right time for the wrong conversation. If someone calls "Red," then the conversation and meeting is ended and rescheduled for another time with perhaps a different approach.

This can even be used as a "huddle conversation" at the start of every shift or in a morning team meeting. Each team member identifies their current mood. Green: "I'm having a good day." Yellow: "There are a few concerns I'm carrying today." Red: "I'm feeling a lot of stress today." Each supervisor, manager, or leader should go first and briefly share some insight into what's behind their choice of color.

It's not therapy nor a time for advice. It's just a quick check in to monitor how emotions might affect the gap between the ideal of the mission, vision, and values and the daily reality of work life for each team member. If the leader is on edge or if the team is on edge, it could displace any effort to live out the *Leadership Development Mission:* "To develop leaders at every level in the entire organization." If leaders lack EQ, if influential team members lack EQ, and/or if the organizational culture lacks EQ, then the mission is compromised, the vision is unattainable, and the development of each employee to achieve their productive potential is no longer feasible. The *Green, Yellow, Red* EQ tool helps build a culture of feedback that facilitates conversations within teams so individuals can offer feedback or feedforward regarding their perception of growth areas needed by supervisors, managers, and leaders who ask.

Reflection—Personal Accountability

Reflection is tied to honest acceptance of candid feedback from a select group of stakeholders. A leader's structured reflection identifies behavioral patterns. This knowledge can reinforce the learning being applied in one's leadership skill set:

» Self-awareness leads to opportunities for personal and professional development. Without personal awareness of our need for continuing development, we hesitate or avoid engagement in moving forward with development planning and accountability to address specific behaviors and competencies.

» Other awareness represents perceptions about you from your work associates who are in a position to identify the blind spots you may not be able or willing to see.

Awareness is the beginning of your personal reality check. It is your key to continued growth as a leader as you look to next steps in your developmental journey. Once we commit to a structured development plan, then we are accountable to participate in structured review and discussion of the learnings from trial-and-error application. It's a process worth pursuing and leads to another cycle of learning and incremental application for each iteration of professional growth and development.

Personal Reflection Tool #1—Your Leadership Development Plan

A simple template will clarify the basics:

1. Identify and describe each focus area to be addressed.

2. Explain why it is important for you to work on each area as part of your professional or career development.

3. Describe the return on investment to your team and to your organization if you further develop each behavior or competency.

4. Provide a summary of the resources you will use for development purposes: Sources for learning, means of interaction regarding the application of learning, and points of application in your current work.

5. Indicate your means of measurement to validate progress.

Personal Reflection Tool #2—Your Reflection Exercise

The following twenty-one-day reflection exercise identifies two questions for each focus area of your leadership development plan. Rate yourself on each question with a simple 1-5 scale. 1 = You blew it today! 5 = You hit the bullseye today! At the end of each day, for twenty-one workdays, send your six personal assessment numbers to your coach, a colleague, or a friend who is supporting you in this development journey. This exercise represents self-accountability toward the goal of sustainable professional development. Here is an adaptation of the tool, as introduced by Marshall Goldsmith:

Ask Daily Questions
The Goldsmith Reflection Exercise and Six Active Questions

"What if you could implement a process that costs almost nothing, takes about three minutes a day, and if you stick with it, will help you achieve your full potential? Would you try it out? The challenge is to ask *Active* questions rather than *Passive* questions which will change the focus of your answers and empower you to make changes you would not otherwise consider... There is a huge difference between 'Do you have clear goals?' and 'Did you do your best to set clear goals for yourself.' The former is trying to determine the individual's state of mind, and the latter challenges the individual to describe and defend a course of action." The following questions are an example from Marshall Goldsmith's daily practice.

1. Did I do my best to increase my happiness?

2. Did I do my best to find meaning?

3. Did I do my best to be engaged?

4. Did I do my best to build positive relationships?

5. Did I do my best to set clear goal?

6. Did I do my best to make progress toward goal achievement?[7]

Asking Your Daily Reflection Questions

It is widely believed that habits take twenty-one days to build into your life. Use the *Goldsmith Reflection Exercise* for twenty-one workdays. Find a friend or colleague who will do this activity with you at the end of every day…each using your own list of six questions. Share your numerical rating for your questions each day for twenty-one days. The accountability is invaluable if you want to improve your leadership effectiveness and efficiency.

Six Development Questions for Daily Reflection (modified by The Leadership Development Group for your use). Use a five-point scale to rate each of your daily questions:

1 = Very Dissatisfied   **2** = Dissatisfied   **3** = Neither   **4** = Satisfied   **5** = Very Satisfied

1. Did I do my best to be aware of my emotional response to each person and situation today and manage if, how, when, where, and to whom to express those emotions?

2. Did I do my best to communicate to my team, vendors, and customers consistently, concisely, and with clarity?

3. Did I do my best to notice the nobodies in spite of my busyness… to help them see their contribution to our mission and vision in any category of employment their position represents?

4. Did I do my best to ask for and receive feedback as to my leadership competency gaps and leadership behaviors that get in the way of leading a high performing team?

5. Did I do my best to practice the reality that leadership is not one of many things I do, but it is everything I do? Did I do everything I could to help my direct reports obtain the information and resources they need to be successful?

6. Did I do my best to adapt my default leadership style to lead in a way that is needed to reshape organizational culture and to achieve our daily mission on the way to reach our preferred future?

Final Thoughts

Consider tracking your twenty-one-day progress on a simple chart with six columns and twenty-one rows. At the end of the twenty-one-day period, average each row and each column of numbers.

> » Your averages of all twenty-one rows will give an indication of your trendline. Are your numbers improving as you go through the exercise or not?

> » Your averages of each of the six columns will tell which of your six questions rated the highest and which rated the lowest.

When leaders commit to this twenty-one-day reflection exercise, the first two weeks of the process are very mechanical, but by week three, they are aware of the questions that are consistently scored lower than seems than appropriate to reach their development goals. That is when the magic happens. That's when new habits begin to be hardwired. This is why it takes twenty-one days.

At a mid-point point in the exercise, the leader will realize the need to start thinking about the six questions at the beginning of each day and not just at the end of the day. Each area of leadership will come into focus as they develop and improve. The process includes: learning, coaching, application, stakeholder feedback, reflection, accountability, and sustainability.

FOURTH WALL CONCLUSION

Connecting the three wires of professional, team, and personal accountability will reinforce the possibility of hardwiring and sustaining the new leadership habits. Development focus areas are identified through the 360-degree interviews and research-based assessments.

» 360-degree feedback and assessments provide the data from which development focus areas are identified.

» A formal development plan charts the "what, why, and how" of your work to strengthen your leadership with new sustainable habits.

» Coaching brings accountability to help a leader think through scenarios of applied learning.

» Credible feedback from a select group of co-workers provides the real-time insight into your progress or lack of progress in continuing leadership development efforts. These stakeholders are making an investment in the sustainability of your new leadership habits.

» The emotional climate of the organization either strengthens a culture of development or inhibits it.

» Self-awareness and other-awareness provide a good check-and-balance process which helps you arrive at conclusions regarding progress and necessary adjustments.

» Structured review and discussion of the learnings from trial-and-error lead to another cycle of learning and incremental application for each iteration of professional growth and development.

In personal reflection,

one looks back to discover

the good and bad of how one

got to where they are.

That journey back

guides one forward,

avoiding future landmines

while leveraging success.

HARDWIRE
CONNECTION #7

PERFECTION OR PROGRESS

Are the development expectations realistic?

» Manageable and Incremental

» Final Thoughts

» Fourth Wall Conclusion

HARDWIRE CONNECTION #7— PERFECTION OR PROGRESS

ARE THE DEVELOPMENT
EXPECTATIONS REALISTIC?

HARDWIRING NEW HABITS is all about focus. It's somewhat overwhelming to look at a leadership competency model with a long list of leadership skills. The Center for Creative Leadership developed their 360 By Design Library of Competencies and Derailment Factors.[1] The list includes over ninety competencies that many HR departments use to formulate their own custom review inventory. It sounds complicated, but this longer list is broken down into four categories and then subcategories within those four that include a final list of specific competencies and derailment factors. Here is a snapshot of their model:

> » Category #1—LEADING OTHERS. This includes Managing Effective Teams, Valuing Diversity, Communicating Effectively, Building and Maintaining Relationships, and Developing Others.

» Category #2—LEADING THE ORGANIZATION. This includes Managing Change, Managing Politics and Influencing Others, Solving Problems and Making Decisions, Taking Risks and Innovating, Setting Vision and Strategy, Enhancing Business Skills and Knowledge, Managing the Work, Understanding and Navigating the Organization.

» Category #3—LEADING YOURSELF. This includes Developing Adaptability, Managing Yourself, Exhibiting Leadership Stature, Demonstrating Ethics and Integrity, Increasing Self-Awareness, Increasing Your Capacity to Learn, Displaying Drive and Purpose.

» Category #4—GLOBAL COMPETENCIES. This includes Decision Maker, Negotiator, Leader, Business Knowledge, Coping, International Business, Perspective Taking, Innovator, Cultural Adaptability.

Manageable and Incremental

The Center for Creative Leadership model provided a starting point that we used to identify our GOR Inc. "Core Competency" list for all leaders. This is where our leadership development work begins. We provide training in the five Core Competency areas: Communication, Change Management, Conflict Resolution, Coaching, and Continuous Improvement. Once people complete this training and the personal action planning that follows, then we identify the "who's who" for coaching by using the New Nine Box Grid. Coaching uses assessments and stakeholder feedback to identify key focus areas for individual growth and development. The criteria we use for coaching is grounded in two qualifiers or filters that are essential to sustainability and hardwiring. First, coaching focus areas must be manageable. Second, the goal must be incremental development.

...Manageable. You can't and shouldn't hardwire the nearly 100 competencies in this model. The goal in development is to narrow your focus to just one to three areas of leadership behaviors or leadership competencies. It's the difference between the prevalent many and the vital few. This means identifying your professional growth criteria to make that final selection. Once you have the list of criteria, then weigh each one as they don't all have equal value or importance in your development or your career planning. When you can identify your vital few, then hardwiring is manageable.

...Incremental. Manageable goals lead to incremental change. We are building a culture of progress, not perfection. Our goal is not that every *team* member will be well-rounded, but that every team is well-rounded. James Clear, author of *Atomic Habits*, says that "Habits are the compound interest of self-improvement." Our short-sighted mistake is trying to do too much too soon. When we take a long-term view, we see the power of compounding effort. It's not only true with our financial investments but also with our investment in developing new leadership habits. In his book, James Clear calculates the compounding effect this way: "If you can get 1 percent better each day for one year, you'll end up thirty-seven times better by the time you're done. Conversely, if you get 1 percent worse each day for one year, you'll decline nearly down to zero...In the beginning, there is basically no difference between making a choice that is 1 percent better or 1 percent worse. (In other words, it won't impact you very much today.) But as time goes on, these small improvements or declines compound and you suddenly find a very big gap between people who make slightly better decisions on a daily basis and those who don't. This is why small choices don't make much of a difference at the time but add up over the long-term."[2]

Incremental Change

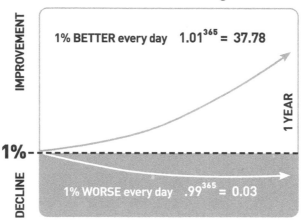

1% BETTER every day $1.01^{365} = 37.78$

1%

1% WORSE every day $.99^{365} = 0.03$

IMPROVEMENT

DECLINE

1 YEAR

Final Thoughts

Manageable and incremental are the rules of the development road. It's
not where you start, but it's where you end up. One of Stephen Covey's
seven habits in his famous book, The *7 Habits for Highly Effective
People*, is to start with the end in mind.[3] It's taking the long-term view
of your professional development. Covey suggests fast forwarding to
the end event of your life. What do you want people to say about you? It
may have more to do with who you are than what you did. Regardless
of how you might answer Covey's question, he invites you to rewind
back to the present day. How will you have to live now for co-workers
to say what you hope they will say at your funeral? Your answer is the
guide of what to focus on to help you become more of who you already
are. This end-of-life exercise is not morbid. It enables you to create a
master list of focus areas for personal and professional development
that is not only manageable but also leads to a series of incremental
changes that compound over a lifetime.

FOURTH WALL CONCLUSION

If you are aiming for perfection in your development, then don't even start! If you want progress toward your productive potential, then focus on a few manageable leadership skills that are vital to your current and future success. Learning and applying new habits are trial-and-error adventures that, at best, lead to incremental change. Remember our 70-20-10 formula: micro learning + macro application = incremental change? When professional development is incremental, then hardwiring new habits is manageable. And when it's manageable, it compounds over time to contribute to the likelihood of sustainability for the long haul.

Development implies change.
There will be stops and starts,
ups and downs, two steps back
and one step forward,
but you can achieve incremental
leadership progress through the
building of new habits.

HARDWIRE CONNECTION #8

AVOID TRIPPING THE TEN CIRCUIT BREAKERS

Are there connection problems that disrupt development?

» Circuit Breakers

» Final Thoughts

» Fourth Wall Conclusion

HARDWIRE CONNECTION #8—
AVOID TRIPPING THE
TEN CIRCUIT BREAKERS

ARE THERE CONNECTION PROBLEMS
THAT DISRUPT DEVELOPMENT?

Circuit Breakers

In the vocabulary of electricity, hardwired is a connection between electrical sources and electronic devices by means of wires. Apply that to organizational leaders. If someone or something is hardwired to do a certain thing, they automatically do it with consistency and cannot change that behavior unless something breaks the connection between learning, application, and hardwiring. In all the Hardwire Connections we have examined, think about what was required to create a development culture that leads to new habits? Consistency is hard enough without being sidetracked by the very things that prevent those new habits from being embedded in every leadership decision and action.

Consider the following "circuit breakers."

1. If every senior leader does not own and model the value of investment in developing supervisors, managers, and leaders at every level of the organization, then the identification of new habits, let alone the sustainability of new habits, is nearly impossible.

2. If values are behaviors and not just ideas to believe, then those behaviors are expected by everyone. No one gets a pass, not the C-Suite, and not the star performers. Hierarchical elitism is never fair. Values as behaviors that shape organizational culture necessitate immediate feedback and consistent accountability for everyone. Those two rules are present in every healthy organization. Without feedback and accountability, even the hardwiring of new leadership habits is compromised.

3. If the organizational mission and vision do not support the developmental mission and vision, then there's not an inspired goal of what all this development effort is leading to. Without clarity of progress toward achieving the identified core outcome, the personal drive to improve and exceed expectations is diminished.

4. If leaders don't address team members in the lower left of the New Nine Box Grid, then it levels the playing field down and never up. If leaders don't include those in the upper right in the strategic thinking of how to achieve the vision, then retention will be a challenge and hardwiring of new leadership habits is rewarded by your competitor.

5. If every employee does not understand the normal and predictable stages of growth or deterioration in the organizational lifecycle, then they'll never have a constructive

view of problems that require change. If team members do not understand that every stage of growth also includes normal and predictable problems unique to that stage, then they will conclude that the organization and its leaders are the problem. Dysfunction in organizations can interfere and take precedence over the value, investment, and execution of a developmental culture for every employee.

6. If leaders don't delegate, then everyone loses. Leaders lose because they don't offload what others on their team could do in order to pay attention to more strategic responsibilities. The team loses because they are never given stretch assignments that contribute to their growth and development. The organization loses because it never reaches its productive potential. Lack of delegation causes a spiral of missed opportunities to develop and equip employees at all levels of the organization.

7. Some leaders don't need or want recognition for what they do. Accomplishment is its own reward, you say? You learned the hard way and so should they? Be careful with these sentiments. The mistake is assuming that everyone on your team is wired the same way. Wrong! Lack of recognition, reward, and celebration de-motivates any desire to grow or to take on more responsibility by those wired differently than you.

8. Among the three levels of a development culture, leading yourself is always harder than leading the team or even leading the organization. If you fail to lead yourself in professional development, then don't expect your team to do it either. Professional development always starts with leading yourself.

9. Being transparent about your best and worst and listening to the perceptions others have of you from a select group of work associates requires personal vulnerability. Sometimes the agenda in development is all about changing perceptions. Leading for the long haul is about adjusting who you are to meet the needs of the organization. Failure to adjust can be a career derailer that ignores needed growth and development.

10. The CliftonStrengths Assessment is a great tool to remind us that as we grow, we don't actually change at the core.[1] Gallup's research shows that as we grow, we become more of who we already are. Family therapist, Virginia Satir, expresses a foundational idea for every company committed to the development of employees at every level in her classic book, *Peoplemaking*: "...living humanly is like...a person who is real and honest to and about himself and others, a person who is willing to take risks, to be creative, to manifest competence, to change when the situation calls for it, and to find ways to accommodate to what is different, keeping that part of the old that is still useful and discarding what is not."[2] What breaks the circuit is trying to be someone other than who you really are. Just be the best you that you can be. Just keep becoming the best that you can become.

Final Thoughts

Antonyms for hardwired: unplanned, accidental, acquired, artificial, careless, disorder, external, flexible, foreign, incidental, negligent, slack, spontaneous, superficial, thoughtless.[3] Use any of the antonyms to describe how the circuit breakers listed above interfere with the sustainability of new leadership habits.

FOURTH WALL CONCLUSION

Hardwiring is hard work! The urgency of meeting protocols, regulations, reaching annual goals, and outperforming your competition always provide the justification to work harder and longer but not always more effectively or more efficiently. Urgency leads to stress and pressure that eats away at the time and resources earmarked for development. We too easily perform according to what is rewarded. In the moment of pressure and stress, we ignore and procrastinate our professional development because we are often just rewarded for getting the urgent job done. The "circuit breaker" is the message heard from senior management: Do more with less. A culture of continual urgency minimizes the value of development in light of an atmosphere that always expects more.

Values, Outcomes, and Development.

*Leadership behavior must
always reflect organizational values.*

*Leadership competency must
always align with strategic outcomes.*

*Leadership development must
always address the behaviors tied
to the outcomes.*

HARDWIRE CONNECTION #9

A COMPARATIVE CASE STUDY

Can Leaders Move from Operations to Strategy?

» Case Study #1

» Case Study #2

» Final Thoughts

» Fourth Wall Conclusion

HARDWIRE CONNECTION #9—
A COMPARATIVE CASE STUDY

CAN LEADERS MOVE FROM
OPERATIONS TO STRATEGY?

Case Study #1

Johan left our company three years ago. He was Director of External Operations for Global Organization Resources. It was a key management position that reported up to Cynthia, the Chief Operations Officer. There had been discussions on promoting Johan to a VP level, but Cynthia didn't feel like he was ready in terms of the leadership skills needed at an executive VP level in our organization. He effectively managed a team of direct reports who coordinated our vendor logistics. That was the "external" part of his job title.

Johan had a great track record. His annual reviews documented how he consistently exceeded expectations in his job performance. Cynthia's perception was that he also had the potential to lead at higher levels of complexity and responsibility but not just yet. He was in the upper right area of the Nine Box Grid, but he had leadership behaviors and competencies that needed further development.

Once Johan realized the VP role was on hold until the next budget cycle, he started to look in the industry for other options. A smaller competitor offered him a VP of Operations role. The difference between our two companies was our commitment to developing employees in every part of the organization. We had the value and made the investment, while the other company had the reputation of "doing more with less." They were stretched thin in their employee benefits, and any effort at retention programs was bare minimum. Career development was not in their vocabulary. "You have a job. Work hard, and we will reward you every payday."

Johan still needed a process to identify and develop his leadership gaps. The deficiencies created frustrations with his new peers, his team, his customers, and ultimately the executive team. At the end of month eleven, it was a mutual parting of ways. He was able to demonstrate exceptional managerial performance in his old job, but the strategic role of senior leadership demanded a different mix of competencies, some of which still needed to be developed. Most competencies, after all, are learned competencies, and Johan had more learning and application to do.

Strategic thinking involves looking around the corner to see what others do not yet see. It's not the formality of developing a strategic plan. It is the ability to think strategically about changes needed that will lead to a new and better tomorrow. It necessitates the ability to do the following:

> » Identify the most relevant data about the industry, market, customer, competition, technology, and even one's employees.

> » Analyze the data to see the reality of the situation in the numbers.

» Synthesize your current state with a realization that you cannot stay the course and keep doing the same things in the same way to get to a better outcome.

» Strategize how to close the gap between your current reality and the required future state.

Johan's story of a career dead-end is tragic. The lack of a development culture in his new company was a career derailer regardless of how much potential he may have had. Two career transitions like these make it difficult to course correct and get back on a pathway to achieve one's leadership potential. Without working in a company that values and invests in the development of employees at every level, there will always be a gap in professional growth and development.

Leadership development is contextual, and organizational culture is the context in which leaders develop. The healthier the organization, the more effective the leader. The healthier the leader, the more effective the organization.

Case Study #2

In the months that followed Johan's departure, Cynthia announced that her retirement was coming in the somewhat near future. She was alerting the organization to the need for succession planning, but it wasn't news to the executive team. They were aware two years previous in their annual workforce planning review. That event is a continual work in progress. Every leader and every manager is asked to update projections on each key role on their team. Stay interviews on every team provided an update on where the company might be vulnerable if expected or unexpected transitions occurred.

The Chief Human Resources Officer was already at work in considering the possibilities of an internal or external candidate to fill Cynthia's role. Simone was identified as an up-and-coming star. We all knew it. Not only did she have the respect of everyone she interfaced with, but people liked her too. She represented what we call the Cinderella Code from a recent 2015 movie version of that memorable story. Before Cinderella's Mom died, she offered her daughter two ideas to guide her life: Have courage and be kind. Simone had both.

The executive team did not make any promises. They understood that an external hire might be necessary, but they acknowledged that an internal candidate would know the culture and the business from day one in the role as Chief Operating Officer. Simone was offered a VP role to work under Cynthia's leadership. As important, she was connected to an external coach to address specific competencies and behaviors needed for senior and strategic leadership.

The coach included an assessment on cognitive style to determine her innate approach to solving operational issues. The coach also completed nine 360-degree interviews with three direct reports, three peers, and three senior leaders. All nine were asked the same four questions:

1. How does Simone already excel as a leader?

2. What is she good at that she needs to get better at in order to lead in even more complex situations?

3. What are Simone's blind spots that get in the way of her interpersonal effectiveness with any level of employee?

4. What leadership best practices does Simone need to add to her leadership toolbox and start using consistently?

The developmental recommendations in the assessment tools and the anecdotal examples of those areas of leadership behavior and competence in the 360-degree interview summary provided one source of what should and could be addressed in the coaching agenda.

The other source that guides all our coaching at the senior level is best summarized in a Harvard Business Review article by Michael D. Watkins from June 2012, titled, "How Managers Become Leaders."[1] The article describes seven seismic shifts that are essential in an individual's move from manager to leader. The shift represents the change in the amount of time and attention given to operations or to strategy. The manager will spend more of their time on operations and less on strategy to accomplish the operation's agenda. The leader will spend most of their time on strategy and a decreasing amount on the operational aspects of their senior role.

What is represented in Watkins' article is recognition that the move from manager to leader changes the focus and skills needed for success.

Seismic Shift #1—**Specialist to Generalist.** Understand the mental models, tools, and terms used in key business functions and develop templates for evaluating the leaders of those functions.

Seismic Shift #2—**Analyst to Integrator.** Integrate the collective knowledge of cross-functional teams and make appropriate trade-offs to solve complex organizational problems.

Seismic Shift #3—**Tactician to Strategist.** Shift fluidly between the details and the larger picture, perceive important patterns in complex environments, and anticipate and influence the reactions of key external players.

Seismic Shift #4—**Bricklayer to Architect.** Understand how to analyze and design organizational systems so that strategy, structure, operating models, and skills fit together effectively. If we harness this understanding, we can make needed organizational changes.

Seismic Shift #5—**Problem Solver to Agenda Setter.** Define the problems the organization should focus on and spot issues that don't fall neatly into any one function but are still important.

Seismic Shift #6—**Warrior to Diplomat.** Proactively shape the environment in which business operates by influencing key external constituencies, including the government, NGOs, the media, and investors.

Seismic Shift #7—**Supporting Cast Member to Lead Role.** Exhibit the right behaviors as a role model for the organization and learn to communicate with and inspire large groups of people directly and indirectly.

The Seven Seismic shifts provide the competency model used in our Leadership Academy at GOR Inc. called, LEAD. It stands for Leaders Encouraged and Developed and is a year-long cohort program. Twenty-four employees at various mid-level to senior-level employment categories participate in the program by invitation only. Each of the seven presentations is followed by a collaborative project that applies the key concepts of each competency area. The LEAD program includes attendance at one world-class external training resource that provides strategic leadership education. Simone faced two challenges in moving from operational manager to strategic leader.

...Hostage to the moment. Operational managers who are subject matter experts are often seen as having potential for promotion to the role of strategic leader. In the early days of making that transition, it is a temptation to default to their subject matter expertise in operational decisions. This leaves little time for strategy. That temptation is tied to the second challenge.

...Do It Yourself. It is hard for operational experts to off-load the things they used to do that someone else on their team could and should be doing. The rationale is perpetuated by dysfunctional thinking: (1) I don't trust my team to do this, (2) I can do it faster...better, (3) I don't have time to train someone to get them up to speed. Delegation is one of the most over-looked skills in strategic leadership. It is a two-step process.

» Step One—Handing off the responsibility for the right person to take ownership for this assignment. This step is the easy step.

» Step Two—Letting go of the authority needed to make decisions and commit organizational resources to the task. This is the step that keeps senior leaders doing more operations and less strategy.

Simone's coach helped her build a Leadership Development Plan to address each of these areas. In twelve months of coaching Simone started hardwiring new habits that focused on strategic leadership. She learned to trust her team in order to delegate to each one in a developmental way that led them through a process to gain the skills needed and the readiness to take on new stretch assignments.

Final Thoughts

Simone did not disappoint anyone. She was recently promoted from VP of Operations to Chief Operating Officer. She is a shining example of professional development working as it should. Read on to see the summary of our analysis. These are the big ideas that supported our Fourth Wall conclusion!

FOURTH WALL CONCLUSION

Once learning leads to application and application leads
to new habitual ways of leading, what is the result? The
return on investment is demonstrated when each leader
is leading a team of people who individually achieve their
own productive potential. Collectively, it makes it possible
for an entire organization to live out its daily mission on the
way to achieving the vision of an inspiring and preferred
future. It is the moment in organizational life that leadership development touches performance, engagement,
satisfaction, attraction, productivity, and retention, all
at once.

Organizational resources invested in your development never guarantee success. It's what you do with those resources that helps you grow further, faster, and for a longer period of time.

HARDWIRE CONNECTION #10

DOES DEVELOPMENT DEVELOP?

Are New Habits Sustainable?

» An Organizational Diagnosis: How Valued is Development?

» A Hardwiring Calculation: How Sustainable Are Your New Leadership Habits?

» The Hardwiring Model: How Does it Happen?

HARDWIRE CONNECTION #10—
DOES DEVELOPMENT DEVELOP?

FOLLOW THE DOLLARS and see the outcome of your company's investment in supervisors, managers, and leaders at all levels, as well as each team member they lead. It's never perfect, but when the trendline shows incremental and continual progress and improvement, it strengthens your answer to the sustainability question. Two final tools will provide a more comprehensive assessment: (1) The Organizational Level—A diagnosis to determine your company's value of and investment in development, and (2) The Individual Level—A calculation of the likelihood of hardwiring your new leadership habits. The Hardwiring Model follows the two assessment tools to provide an overview of our Fourth Wall Assumptions.

An Organizational Diagnosis:
How Valued is Development?

①	②	③	④	⑤	⑥	⑦	⑧	⑨	⑩

Uncertainty of mission, vision, value — or — Clarity of mission, vision, values

No development pathway exists here — or — We value and guide in professional development

Employee disengagement — or — Employee engagement

Employee dissatisfaction — or — Employee satisfaction

Too many people miss expectations — or — Most people meet or exceed expectations

Team silos — or — Team collaboration

"It's good enough" — or — We strive to achieve our org's productive potential

"We've always done it that way" — or — We are committed to continual improvement

Leaders are the exception to the rule — or — Leaders model the way

"Just hire someone soon" — or — We have a leadership pipeline

Score each line (1 to 10) based on your experience and perspective. Then add up your final overall number. The higher your total number, the more likely that you are working in an organization that operationalizes the value of developing team members at every level. The lower your total number, the more likely that the organization, in its very core, is inhibiting the possibility of developing team members at every level of the company.

A Hardwiring Calculation:
How Sustainable Are Your New Leadership Habits?

①	②	③	④	⑤	⑥	⑦	⑧	⑨	⑩

Only external learning opportunities	— or —	Numerous internal learning opportunities
I learn just to know more	— or —	I incrementally apply what I learn
What is a career plan?	— or —	I have a career plan
Mission/Vision are management's ideas	— or —	What I do contributes to the mission and vision
My values don't match the org's values	— or —	I'm committed to our org's values
I am in the lower left of Nine Box Grid	— or —	I am in the upper right of the Nine Box Grid
I don't fit in with the culture here	— or —	The culture fits my values, motives, and preferences
No development conversations	— or —	Regular proactive development conversations
I never like getting feedback	— or —	I have a few colleagues whom I ask and listen to
The list to work on is too long	— or —	I focus on a few things for incremental development

Score each line (1-10) based on your experience and perspective. Then add up your final overall number. The higher your total number, the more likely is your potential to hardwire new leadership habits. The lower your total number, the greater the probability that change will be unsustainable.

THE HARDWIRING MODEL

LEADERSHIP DEVELOPMENT FOUNDATIONS

Shaping Organizational Culture

— **Value • Invest • Operationalize • Equip** —

LEADERSHIP DEVELOPMENT PATHWAYS

Clarifying Individual Focus

— **Plan • Learn • Apply** —

LEADERSHIP DEVELOPMENT HARDWIRING

Sustaining New Leadership Habits

— **Coaching • Feedback • Reflection • Incremental Change** —

Leadership Development Foundations—When organizations value and invest in leadership development, it defines the very core of its culture. It leads to operationalizing that value and providing the resources needed to equip every supervisor, manager, and leader for career conversations with direct reports. Development is a shared value when modeled at each level of employment.

Leadership Development Pathways—When organizations establish a core competency model for every supervisor, manager, and leader, it creates an intentional focus for each team member committed to professional growth. It leads to the creation of individual devlopment plans, learning strategies, and the accountability to apply new learning. It's all about doing the work you are already doing...differently.

Leadership Development Hardwiring—When organizations advocate and support the development of leaders, it enhances the sustainability of new leadership habits. It leads to coaching for external accountability, feedback from key stakeholders for team accountability, and self-reflection for personal accountability. Leaders achieve incremental change in specific leadership skills and competencies.

FOURTH WALL REVIEW:
NINE HARDWIRED CONNECTIONS

Hardwire Connection #1—Pathways to Development

The analysis in Hardwire Connection #1 brings us closer to understanding how the development journey begins. When a leader has clarity on specific leadership behaviors or competencies that need attention, then the development journey begins through structured and applied learning translated into new habits in how one leads. Learning is where hardwiring begins. Learning without application is merely an academic exercise with no meaningful return on investment for the business at large. We are aware that there will always be team members at GOR Inc. who take advantage of learning opportunities but may never translate that learning into new ways of supervising, managing, and leading. That is one of our challenges going forward. The purpose of learning in our thinking is to continue one's development in order to provide more effective leadership with maximum impact and efficiency. That initial idea in our analysis begins to shape our Fourth Wall Conclusion.

Hardwire Connection #2—Organizational Enablers

Hardwire Connection #2 continues our C-Suite team's research and analysis of what is needed to clarify the context of leadership development at Global Organization Resources Inc. We are applying the ideas of mission, vision, and values from an organizational level specifically to our company's work in developing every supervisor, manager, and leader.

The three organizational enablers—mission...vision...values—bring clarity to the work of leadership development. They apply to leaders at every level of the organization. They contribute to an internal pipeline of developing supervisors, managers, and leaders who continue to invest in the strengthening of their competence in order to enhance their own leadership capacity. As leaders model professional growth, they are also investing in the development of each of their direct reports.

Cultural fit is the question to ask long before asking the development question. It is an essential filter to use in the hiring process. It's not just about performance, potential, and personal drive. Hiring also considers one's fit within the culture of how we work together with other employees, vendors, customers, investors, and even competitors. "If we hire you, will we like you (character) and will we also respect you (competence)?" Development never fixes fit. If you don't fit, then hardwiring new leadership habits is a waste of time.

The return on investment from clarifying the mission, vision, and values in leadership development is the long-term protection of the organization's viability in seasons of employee retirement or workforce turnover.

> » Mission—We are committed to develop leaders at every level of the company.

> » Vision—We have a succession planning pipeline from the company's talent pool.

> » Values—We pay attention to character, competence, capacity, and the cultural fit of every team member.

Hardwire Connection #3—The Who's Who Matrix

As we considered performance, potential, and personal drive related to one's developmental potential in Hardwire Connection #3, our team came to the following insights and conclusions:

> » For those in the lower left of the New Nine Box Grid, development may not develop them. If it doesn't, then the difficult question of whether to release and replace them confronts the leader for the sake of the rest of the team. Not dealing with the lower left has a negative impact on the development of every other team member.

» For those in the middle of the grid or in the upper right, the potential for development leading to higher levels of responsibility is measured by the combination of past performance, perceived future potential, and especially personal drive.

» Performance that exceeds expectations and potential that allows one to stand out is based, in part, on the perceptions of others. The validity of those perceptions is strengthened by feedback from a cross section of employees who interface regularly with the individual and come to similar conclusions. Look for the development themes mentioned by two or more. Ignore the outlier comment from just one team member. Perceptions help establish the developmental agenda for each employee. They provide anecdotal examples of what may show up as developmental recommendations in a variety of assessment tools.

» Does development develop? Yes, typically, but not always in the same way for everyone! The development agenda is unique to each box on the New Nine Box Grid, and it is dynamic within a healthy organizational culture where every team member has absolute clarity on the mission, vision, and values. Whatever is needed to move each team member toward the upper right area of the grid is part of their agenda for further development.

» The New Nine Box Grid provides a tool to assess the performance, potential, and personal drive of each supervisor, manager, and leader. The intention is to move them to the upper right section of the grid, which implies hardwiring to enhance new competencies and behaviors. Without a development plan resulting from that annual assessment, the natural tendency is to slip further away from the upper right. Without a plan, learning is not always applied. Without application, new habits are not hardwired.

Hardwire Connection #4—It All Happens on Three Levels

Developmental organizations make developmental teams possible. Developmental teams make developing individuals possible. When all three intersect and work together toward the same mission, vision, and values, then the probability of hardwiring new leadership habits increases.

The organization is critical.

The team is essential.

The individual is non-negotiable.

People can't achieve individual progress without the team leader encouraging and supporting each of their direct reports. Team leaders can't effectively lead the way for the development of each direct report if the organization doesn't value a development culture. Organizations aren't really committed to the value of development unless they invest, with the right mindset and real dollars, in what is needed to make that value a reality for every employee at every level of the organization.

Hardwire Connection #5—When Learning Is Applied

Micro learning from a variety of sources lends itself to macro application of new leadership insights. Self-reflection is a deliberate, honest, and objective review of your thoughts, feelings, emotions, and changes in your existing leadership habits. Feedback from a trusted group of colleagues corrects your personal bias and refines your clarity on what to apply and how to apply it. Even the smallest incremental change compounded over time can contribute to new habitual ways of leading.

Our review and discussion of the insights in Hardwire Connection #5 challenged our investment in leadership development resources. We all agree that learning without application is a waste of organizational resources. When application develops new habitual ways of leading that are hardwired, then leadership effectiveness and efficiency improves and organizational performance is enhanced.

Hardwire Connection #6—Connecting Three Wires

Connecting the three wires of professional, team, and personal accountability will reinforce the probability of hardwiring and sustaining the new leadership habits. Development focus areas are identified through the 360-degree interviews and research-based assessments.

» 360-degree feedback and assessments provide the data from which development focus areas are identified.

» A formal development plan charts the "what, why, and how" of your work to strengthen your leadership with new sustainable habits.

» Coaching brings accountability to help a leader think through scenarios of applied learning.

» Credible feedback from a select group of co-workers provides the real-time insight into your progress or lack of progress in continuing leadership development efforts. These stakeholders are making an investment in the sustainability of your new leadership habits.

» The emotional climate of the organization either strengthens a culture of development or inhibits it.

» Self-awareness and other-awareness provide a good check-and-balance process which helps you arrive at conclusions regarding progress and necessary adjustments.

» Structured review and discussion of the learnings from trial-and-error lead to another cycle of learning and incremental application for each iteration of professional growth and development.

Hardwire Connection #7—Perfection or Progress

If you are aiming for perfection in your development, then don't even start! If you want progress toward your productive potential, then focus on a few manageable leadership skills that are vital to your current and future success. Learning and applying new habits is a trial-and-error adventure that, at best, leads to incremental change. Remember our 70-20-10 formula: micro learning + macro application = incremental change? When professional development is incremental, then hardwiring new habits is manageable. And when it's manageable, it compounds over time to contribute to the likelihood of sustainability for the long haul.

Hardwire Connection #8—Avoid Tripping the Ten Circuit Breakers

Hardwiring is hard work! The urgency of meeting protocols, regulations, reaching annual goals, and outperforming your competition always provide the justification to work harder and longer but not always more effectively or more efficiently. Urgency leads to stress and pressure that eats away at the time and resources earmarked for development. We too easily perform according to what is rewarded. In the moment of pressure and stress, we ignore and procrastinate our professional development because we are often just rewarded for getting the urgent job done. The "circuit breaker" is the message heard from senior management: Do more with less. A culture of continual urgency minimizes the value of development in light of an atmosphere that always expects more.

Hardwire Connection #9—A Comparative Case Study

Once learning leads to application and application leads to new habitual ways of leading, what is the result? The return on investment is demonstrated when each leader is leading a team of people who individually achieve their own productive potential. Collectively, it makes it possible for an entire organization to live out its daily mission on the way to achieving the vision of an inspiring and preferred future. It is the moment in organizational life that leadership development touches performance, engagement, satisfaction, attraction, productivity, and retention, all at once.

Hardwire Connection #10—Does Development Develop?

Follow the dollars and see the outcome of your company's investment in supervisors, m anagers, and leaders at all levels, as well as each team member they lead. It's never perfect, but when the trendline shows incremental and continual progress and improvement, it strengthens your answer to the sustainability question.

DOES DEVELOPMENT DEVELOP?

Not perfectly Not for everyone

BUT NEW LEADERSHIP HABITS ARE MORE LIKELY TO BE HARDWIRED **WHEN...**

The Fourth Wall

...WHEN YOUR COMPANY **VALUES + INVESTS** IN THE DEVELOPMENT OF TEAM MEMBERS

...WHEN YOUR COMPANY CREATES A PATHWAY TO DEVELOPMENT FOR EVERY **SUPERVISOR, MANAGER,** AND **LEADER**

...WHEN LEADERS HAVE THE **PERSONAL DRIVE** TO KEEP **GETTING BETTER**

...WHEN THE COMPANY'S CULTURE IS **DEVELOPMENTAL** AT ITS CORE

...WHEN **LEARNING** IS EXPECTED TO LEAD TO APPLICATION

...WHEN LEADERS ARE WILLING TO BE **ACCOUNTABLE** TO A COACH AND TO THE STAKEHOLDERS ON THEIR TEAM

...WHEN THE **MISSION, VISION** AND **VALUES** INCLUDE A COMMITMENT TO DEVELOPING LEADERS AT ALL LEVELS

...WHEN **DEVELOPMENT** IS BOTH MANAGEABLE AND INCREMENTAL

...WHEN THE **DEVELOPMENT SKEPTIC** IS CONVINCED BY THE DATA THAT TELLS THE **FULL STORY**

...WHEN THE NEW **NINE BOX GRID** CHARTS THOSE IN THE UPPER RIGHT AND CLARIFIES THOSE IN THE LOWER LEFT WHO LOWER NOT LEVEL THE PLAYING FIELD

...WHEN DEVELOPMENT IS MORE ABOUT **PROGRESS** AND LESS ABOUT **PERFECTION**

...WHEN LEADERS IN A DEVELOPMENT PROCESS **TAKE TIME** FOR REFLECTION TO ASSESS PROGRESS AND TO IDENTIFY CHANGES NEEDED IN THE NEXT ITERATION OF LEARNING AND APPLICATION

The Leadership Core

*Shaping leadership character
results in positive influence with
those you lead.*

*Investing in leadership competence
results in effective action
with those you lead.*

*Stretching leadership capacity
results in maximizing the productive
potential of those you lead.*

ABOUT THE AUTHOR

Dr. Dick Daniels is a leadership strategist with a passion to help leaders achieve their productive potential by leading their teams and organizations more effectively and efficiently. Dr. D hosts The Leadership Development Group on LinkedIn with more than 90,000 global leadership practitioners following the weekly conversation about best practice insights on developing leaders at all levels in any organization.

His nationally awarded books include *Leadership Briefs: Shaping Organizational Culture to Stretch Leadership Capacity* and *Leadership Core: Character, Competence, Capacity.* In addition, his chapter, "Leadership Musings," was included in the 2019 Building Bridges series at the International Leadership Association. The book, *Leadership and Power in International Development*, won the R. Wayne Pace Human Resource Book of the Year by the Academy for Human Resource Development. Dick has also written a trilogy of nationally awarded children's picture books titled, Oak Street Treehouse.

Dr. D is the Vice President of Consulting Services for Right Management Florida Caribbean. He serves as a Facilitator with the Chief Executive Network and is Founder and President of The Leadership Development Group. As a member of the Hodos Institute Board, he provides guidance in their leadership development research and initiatives throughout Eurasia.

ACKNOWLEDGMENTS:

Heidi Sheard has once again added her editing expertise to take the final copy to a better place. Her attention to my intent in writing adds clarity and is always more concise than my rambling, conversational style. She has been the final word in all three leadership books, and I am grateful for the questions she raises and the ideas she suggests with the reader in mind. Thanks, Heidi! Kendal Marsh at The Brand Office has provided the cover design as well as the interior layout and design on all three leadership volumes. His design magic transforms an ordinary page of words in a way that stimulates the eye as well as the mind. His team at The Brand Office brings a depth and breadth to creativity for each project. Thanks, Kendal!

Dr. D...
Dick Daniels
The Leadership Development Group

ENDNOTES

HARDWIRE CONNECTION #1

1. Lang, Lisa, "Enter the Learning Zone," *TD Magazine*, Association for Talent Development, April 2022, page 32.

2. International Coaching Federation (ICF), www.coachingfederation.org, access date, July 22, 2022.

3. American Psychological Association, https://www.apa.org/ed/graduate/specialize/counseling#:~:text=Counseling%20Psychology%20is%20a%20generalist,and%20increase%20their%20ability%20to, access date June 7, 2022.

HARDWIRE CONNECTION #4

1. Oxford Reference, "Curator," https://www.oxfordreference.com/view/10.1093/acref/9780199661350.001.0001/acref-9780199661350-e-1269, access date June 7, 2022.

2. Grady, James, *A Simple Statement: A Guide to Nonprofit Arts Management and Leadership*, (Heinemann Drama: Portsmouth, NH, 2006).

3. Search Institute, https://www.search-institute.org/our-research/development-assets/developmental-assets-framework/, access date July 28, 2022.

4. Paulson, Terry L., *They Shoot Managers, Don't They: Managing Yourself and Leading Others in a Changing World*, (Ten Speed Press: Santa Monica CA, 1988,) page 104.

5. Society for Human Resource Management, https://www.shrm.org/resourcesandtools/tools and samples/hr-forms/pages/stayinterviewquestions.aspx, access date, July 27, 2022.

6. Green, Bill, "Building a Company Culture That Is Fast and Efficient Starts With the Founder," *Inc. Magazine*, https://www.inc.com/bill-green/the-speed-of-boss-is-speed-of-team-heres-why-founders-need-to-set-pace.html, June 26, 2018, access date, June 24, 2022.

7. Luft, Joe and Ingram, Harry, "The Johari Window, a Graphic Model of Interpersonal Awareness," Proceedings of the Western Training Laboratory in Group Development. (UCLA: Los Angeles, 1955).

HARDWIRE CONNECTION #5

1. Center for Creative Leadership, "The 70-20-10 Rule for Leadership Development," https://www.ccl.org/articles/leading-effectively-articles/70-20-10-rule/, access date, May 13, 2022.

2. Lombardo, Michael M, Eichinger, Robert, *Career Architect Development Planner*, (Lominger Limited: Minneapolis, 1996).

HARDWIRE CONNECTION #6

1. The Proctor Gallager Institute, "Accountability," https://www.proctorgallagherinstitute.com/17557/accountability, access date, July 28, 2022.

2. Newland, Stephen, "The Power of Accountability," https://www.afcpe.org/news-and-publications/the-standard/2018-3/the-power-of-accountability/, 3rd quarter 2018, access date, May 30, 2022.

3. Institute of Coaching: McLean, Affiliate of Harvard Medical School, "Benefits of Coaching," https://instituteofcoaching.org/coaching-overview/coaching-benefits, access date, July 20, 2022.

4. LinkedIn, "Brandon Mergard," "The Role of Time in Executive Coaching Effectiveness," June 2019, https://www.linkedin.com/in/brandonjamesmergard/recent-activity/, access date, August 15, 2022.

5. Hogan Assessments, https://www.hoganassessments.com/, access date, July 26, 2022.

6. Goldsmith, Marshall, "Try Feedforward Instead of Feedback," https://marshallgoldsmith.com/articles/try-feedforward-instead-feedback/, access date, July 26, 2022.

7. Goldsmith, Marshall, "Question That Make a Difference," https://marshallgoldsmith.com/articles/questions-that-make-a-difference-the-daily-question-process/, access date, July 22, 2022.

HARDWIRE CONNECTION #7

1. "360 By Design® Library of Competencies and Derailment Factors," https://docplayer.net/21027017-360-by-design-library-of-competencies-and-derailment-factors.html, access date, August 15, 2022.

2. Clear, James, *Atomic Habits: An Easy & Proven Way to Build Good Habits & Break Bad Ones*, (Avery Publishing: New York City, 2018).

3. Covey, Steven, *The 7 Habits of Highly Effective People*, (Simon & Schuster: New York City, 2020).

HARDWIRE CONNECTION #8

1. Gallup, "CliftonStrengths Assessment," https://www.gallup.com/cliftonstrengths/en/252137/home.aspx, access date, July 26, 2022.

2. Satir, Virginia, *Peoplemaking*, (Souvenir Press: Chicago, 1990), page 2.

3. Power Thesaurus, "Antonyms for Hardwired," https://www.powerthesaurus.org/hardwired/antonyms, access date, July 27, 2022.

HARDWIRE CONNECTION #9

1. Watkins, Michael D., "How Managers Become Leaders," *Harvard Business Review*, June 2012, https://hbr.org/2012/06/how-managers-become-leaders, access date July 9, 2022.

INDEX

C